The Complete Guide to Behaviour for Teaching Assistants and Support Staff

The Complete Guide to Behaviour for Teaching Assistants and Support Staff

Chris Lee

SAGE

Los Angeles | London | New Delhi
Singapore | Washington DC

SAGE Publications Ltd
1 Oliver's Yard
55 City Road
London EC1Y 1SP

SAGE Publications Inc.
2455 Teller Road
Thousand Oaks, California 91320

SAGE Publications India Pvt Ltd
B 1/I 1 Mohan Cooperative Industrial Area
Mathura Road
New Delhi 110 044

SAGE Publications Asia-Pacific Pte Ltd
33 Pekin Street #02-01
Far East Square
Singapore 048763

Library of Congress Control Number. 2010923537

British Library Cataloguing in Publication data

A catalogue record for this book is available from
the British Library

ISBN 978 1 84787 583 9
ISBN 978 1 84787 584 6 (pbk)

Typeset by C&M Digitals (P) Ltd, Chennai, India
Printed by CPI Antony Rowe, Chippenham, Wiltshire
Printed on paper from sustainable resources

Contents

List of exercises, figures and tables

Exercises

Figures

Tables

Abbreviations

DCSF   Department for Children, Schools and Families

DfES   Department for Education and Skills

HLTA   Higher Level Teaching Assistant

NASSP   National Association of Secondary School Principals

NOS   National Occupational Standards

SEAL   Social and Emotional Aspects of Learning

SEN   Special Educational Needs

TA   Teaching Assistant

TDA   Teacher Development Agency

Acknowledgements

I am indebted to all those who have assisted in the writing of this book, especially support and care staff of the Novalis Trust and Dawlish Community College with whom I have worked for many years. Individual thanks should go to Shan Greene, Miriam Chadwick, Caroline Littler, Chris Trengrove, Melissa Miggin, Kerry White-Cheshire, Diane Holdsworth, Jackie Carpenter, Rachel Guy, Sarah Seymour, Nicky Noble, Amy Greenhill and Nann Stimpson. I should like to dedicate the book to all the teaching assistants and other care and support staff who have attended conferences and courses presented by me and who have informed and helped to develop the ideas herein.

About the author

Chris Lee was, until recently, Senior Lecturer in Education and Head of the School of Continuing Professional Development at the Faculty of Education, University of Plymouth. He has taught in secondary and special schools, and continues to work with teachers on issues of bullying and behaviour management. He is now a freelance educational consultant and undertakes training and support for teaching assistants in all types of school.

1

The context

This opening chapter describes what the book does and also underlines the importance of skills, values and beliefs to the work of teaching assistants (TAs) and other support staff in schools and other educational settings in dealing with difficult behaviour from pupils. It is followed by an overview of current developments for TAs and their changing role plus a consideration of the value of the book to staff working towards Teacher Development Agency (TDA) standards. There is a discussion of the advantages and disadvantages of being a Teaching Assistant when pupils are being disruptive which is illustrated by quotations from those who know best – the TAs themselves.

What this book is about

This book will help teaching assistants (TAs) and other support staff working in schools and colleges to increase their understanding and skills in preventing and dealing with disruptive or difficult behaviour. Occasionally books of this type aim to tell the reader what to do, as if a special technique will always work. This is not a book that tells the TA how to behave in situations but rather it presents a model of the TA who is able to operate successfully in various ways and in numerous contexts. In addition to discussing ways of preventing behaviour difficulties it develops all three major approaches to behaviour management by focusing on the school system, the importance of negotiating or contracting with pupils and the key skills that support and enhance relationships in schools. The book offers many ideas built around a simple principle – the more skills and ideas the TA possesses the more likely they are to be successful in preventing and dealing with difficult situations. However, I hope these ideas are not presented in what can often feel like a patronising 'do this because it will work' style: they are underpinned by case studies, lists and exercises that help individual and groups of support staff to consider what works for them and what might not. There is also an ongoing consideration of the role and status of TAs and support staff in their schools as any book which presents ideas that do not resonate with the values, roles and skills of the TA and the school in which they work will be of limited value. Based upon ideas initially expressed in one of my chapters in *A Toolkit for the Effective Teaching Assistant* (Lee, 2009), it is book that invites more than a cursory glance but rather welcomes working through as part of any personal reflection or professional development scheme.

Who it is designed for

The initial idea for this book originated while I was working with teaching assistants and other support staff who were studying on Foundation Degree programmes. 'Behaviour Management' was a module that was studied on their course and it became apparent that it was also a major area in which TAs wished to develop their skills. Since starting my career as a freelance consultant this demand from TAs for enhancing their knowledge and skills has become even more evident. Throughout this book the main term employed for those for whom it is designed is teaching assistant, referred to throughout as TA, but use is also made of the term support staff which includes those working under the title 'care staff'.

The book is designed to enhance knowledge and understanding of:

- TAs;

- care and support staff in an educational setting;

- TAs seeking to meet the National Occupational Standards (NOS) for supporting teaching and learning in schools;

- TAs seeking to meet the Higher Level Teaching Assistant (HLTA) standards;

- those who have the challenging task of teaching classes in the absence of teachers, i.e. cover supervisors;

- students studying on Foundation Degrees in education or related areas;

- students studying to be teachers;

- teachers, especially those who have a responsibility for professional development in their schools and provide programmes for any of the above.

However, the principal target audience remains those who work with children and young people in any form of supportive role and are not teachers.

Overview

One of the major areas of change in schools over the last ten years is the rise in the numbers of TAs and other forms of support staff in school. Accompanying that increase has been a greater diversity of role, increasing status through the HLTA programme and more direct involvement in teaching classes and groups through cover supervisors. In addition, there are increased opportunities for professional development and study. With these developments there have been accompanying changes in role and function for teaching assistants. Job descriptions for TAs usually start with a list of tasks that follow the word 'support', e.g. 'support the plans of the teacher', 'support the assessment policy'. Until recent times, teachers have been clear that they are in charge of the learning in the classroom and the behaviour of the pupils that secured the climate in which that learning took place. TAs supported the practices of the teacher as well as the learning of the pupils and enforcement of the policies of the school. However, the modern classroom is experiencing turbulence which has been influenced if not directed by government initiatives such as 'Workforce Reform', 'Extended Schools' and 'Every Child Matters'. The concept of the school day, the relationship between educationalists and other caring professions and even what it means to be a teacher or a member of the support staff is being redefined. This reform agenda has also changed the landscape for TAs as they have found new pedagogic responsibilities through the HLTA and with that comes increased expectations of the HLTA status as a classroom manager. The notion of the TA as a general assistant to the teacher contributing wherever possible to the lesson still exists but increasingly skilful and targeted provision has resulted in TAs undertaking a complex set of tasks and assuming greater responsibility than has hitherto been the case. This is reflected in the TDA National Occupational Standards accompanying these developments, and in the increasing involvement of TAs with all aspects of school life including the behaviour of pupils with the attendant stresses that accompany the task. It has always been the case that inappropriate or disruptive behaviour has been picked up by TAs but in the modern school they are more than ever involved in dealing with these forms of behaviour directly. This book is designed to support them in that task.

The demand for TAs to increase their skills in both preventing and dealing with behaviour problems is becoming the same as teachers. Both roles demand a range of skills, few of which can be taught and most of which are acquired through experience. However, the TA has a major disadvantage over their teaching counterpart. They often lack the status and, therefore, probably the power that comes with the status that teachers possess. There is natural authority built into the role of the teacher, although it could be argued that this is not as prevalent in modern schools as it used to be. Certainly teachers can rarely rely solely upon their status to deal with difficult situations. In not having the natural authority of the teacher, TAs may be disadvantaged but they also may have two advantages. First, some pupils may deliberately rebel against the authority of the teacher and, second, in not possessing such imposing authority, TAs are compelled to look for other ways of dealing with difficulties. They have to be creative and flexible using every technique and idea in their armoury. Some of them have a third advantage in that their knowledge of certain pupils means that they will be able to draw upon that closeness of relationship to deal with a situation. Much here will depend upon their role being related to specific pupils or groups rather than general classroom tasks, their knowledge of a variety of techniques as well as maybe more time to observe and listen to pupils. Whatever their status and role all support staff benefit from possessing a range of skills for coping with disruption and maybe more challenging forms of behaviour.

The structure of the book

This chapter focuses on the role of the TA and reflects upon the advantages and disadvantages that go with that role. Chapter 2 considers what can be done to prevent classroom disruption or problems with individual pupils with whom the TA works closely. The remaining chapters introduce and elaborate on the three broad approaches to dealing with behaviour problems. The three approaches are described as:

- the system approach;

- the negotiation approach;

- the relationship approach.

These approaches are the full spectrum of professional skills available to the TA and in this sense it is the 'complete' range. They are **not** centred on the problems that the pupils may present, although there is some consideration of these, but the focus is on **the skills, values and beliefs** that are held by the person who deals with the problem – the TA. Beliefs are crucial to how you perceive what is happening with your pupils and the book places emphasis on how events are interpreted and understood and, therefore, how you respond to those events.

All the chapters contain objectives for the chapter in a brief opening section and there are many exercises for TAs to undertake. While the exercises can be undertaken on your own – indeed they are designed for individual reflection – there are benefits to undertaking them in groups and discussing the outcomes and implications for your practice. Additionally, each chapter contains references and points to additional reading that will support further study and investigation.

Terminology

The language used to describe behaviour that can cause problems in schools is in itself a problem and mention should be made of the terms employed in the book. Terms such as 'difficult behaviour' and 'disruptive behaviour' have been included but no matter what phrases are used there are problems that are attached to them. For example, with 'inappropriate behaviour' who defines behaviour as 'inappropriate'? Is it the case that teaching assistants and teachers are always the judges of what is inappropriate? Much the same could be said of 'disruptive'. Throughout the book the terms used have been chosen because they are often used by TAs and ones which they appear to be comfortable with. Every attempt has been made to avoid labelling the pupil; it is their behaviour that presents us with difficulties, not the pupil.

The behaviour that causes problems is that which interferes with the learning of others and staff rights to teach their lessons. It may be low-level disruption aiming to unsettle the equilibrium of a settled learning group or it may be disturbing for classmates and threaten their feelings of security or, more challengingly, it may be that which threatens the social order of the class or the school.

Meeting Standards

This book has been written as a stand-alone text that enhances professional understanding and development in a variety of areas of behaviour management in the various settings where learning takes place, but especially schools. However, it has a number of uses for those who are seeking formal qualifications and undertaking study and practice based upon centrally developed ideas and the following are just illustrations of its potential.

The Teacher Development Agency (TDA) has brought together a number of the National Occupational Standards (NOS) (www.tda.gov. uk/support/nos) that inform or determine the effectiveness of the many aspects of assistance, care and support in all key educational settings. They also include settings such as Management of Volunteers, Health and Social Care and Information and Library Services. The Standards are divided into Units which are based upon the roles and responsibilities of support staff in schools and are structured in the same way as the former National Occupational Standards for Teaching Assistants in that there are Core and Optional Units at Level 2 and Level 3. This book will help support staff to achieve a variety of standards and the specific core unit at Level 3 which addresses behaviour matters, STL19 *Promote positive behaviour*, more on this on the next page. It may be that it helps in addressing a number of standards not mentioned below but those included are the more obvious cases.

I hope this book helps TAs to reflect on their practice and to consider their own values that may be challenging and, therefore, is likely to step beyond meeting the Standards. However, it does make a useful contribution to achieving many of them and will prove a key source of ideas for those seeking to address any Standards broadly related to behaviour management and pupil well-being.

The Higher Level Teaching Assistants (HLTA) Standards (www.tda.gov. uk/support/hlta) have one direct reference to behaviour management:

26. *Use effective strategies to promote positive behaviour*

but have a number of other relevant standards such as:

  2. *Establish fair, respectful, trusting, supportive and constructive rela-tionships with children and young people*

As mentioned before, for a more intensive and detailed consideration of how this book can help in meeting standards Table 1.1 illustrates the link to the specific National Occupational Standard Level 3 Core Unit STL19: *Promote positive behaviour* which includes such requirements as:

19.1 *Implement agreed behaviour management strategies*

and:

19.2 *Support pupils in taking responsibility for their learning and behaviour*

However, there are many chapters in this book which will support achieving particular performance criteria and it would be wrong to suggest that the above is the only unit that the book will help in achieving. It is important to emphasise that such is the link between learning and behaviour that there are very few units that the key ideas in this book would *not* address. Those selected below are the more obvious cases and include:

Level 2 Core STL4: *Contribute to positive relationships*
Level 3 Core ST20: *Develop and promote positive relationships*
Level 3 Optional STL37: *Contribute to the prevention and management of challenging behaviour in children and young people*
Level 3 Optional STL41: *Support pupils with behaviour, emotional and social needs*
Level 3 Optional STL45: *Promote children's well-being and resilience*
Level 3 Optional STL48: *Support young people in tackling problems and taking action.*

Table 1.1 Promote positive behaviour

Performance criteria	Chapter
19.1 P1 apply agreed behaviour management strategies fairly and consistently at all times	2–7
19.1 P2 provide an effective role model for the standards of behaviour expected of pupils and adults within the school	1–7
19.1 P3 provide praise and encouragement to pupils to recognise and promote positive pupil behaviour in line with school policies	4
19.1 P4 use appropriate strategies to minimise disruption through inappropriate behaviour	2–7
19.1 P5 regularly remind pupils of the school's code of conduct	3
19.1 P6 take immediate action to deal with any bullying, harassment or oppressive behaviour in accordance with your role and responsibilities	2–6
19.1 P7 recognise and respond appropriately to risks to yourself and/or others during episodes of challenging behaviour	2–6
19.1 P8 refer incidents of inappropriate behaviour outside your area of responsibility to the relevant staff member for action	2–3
19.1 P9 contribute to reviews of behaviour, including bullying, attendance and the effectiveness of rewards and sanctions, as relevant to your role	4
19.1 P10 provide clear and considered feedback on the effectiveness of behaviour management strategies	1–7
19.2 P1 encourage pupils to take responsibility for their own learning and behaviour when working on their own, in pairs, in groups and in whole-class situations	5–6
19.2 P2 use peer and self-assessment techniques to increase pupils' involvement in their learning and promote good behaviour	5-6
19.2 P3 highlight and praise positive aspects of pupils' behaviour	4
19.2 P4 recognise patterns and triggers which may lead to inappropriate behavioural responses and take appropriate action to pre-empt problems	5
19.2 P5 encourage and support pupils to consider the impact of their behaviour on others, themselves and their environment	5–6

Table 1.1 (Continued)

Performance criteria	Chapter
19.2 P6 support pupils with behaviour difficulties to identify and agree on ways in which they might change or manage their behaviour to achieve desired outcomes	5–6
19.2 P7 support pupils in a manner which is likely to make them feel valued and respected and recognises progress made	5–6
19.2 P8 encourage and support pupils to regularly review their own behaviour, attitude and achievements	5–6
19.2 P9 contribute to collecting data on pupils' attendance and behaviour, including the use of rewards and sanctions, to inform policy review and planning	3–4
19.2 P10 provide feedback to relevant people on progress made by any pupils with a behaviour support plan	2–3

The advantages of being a teaching assistant/member of support staff

At the heart of the book is the central argument that TAs benefit from a breadth of ideas, skills and techniques in dealing with difficult pupil behaviour. This view is supported by TAs themselves when asked what the advantages are of being a TA when it comes to dealing with difficult classroom behaviour. Analysis of their statements reveals a belief in their closeness to the pupils and the opportunity that a more flexible role presents in dealing with situations usually before they begin to disrupt others, including the time to intervene. Many comments also reflect a perceived personal role that support staff can play between teachers and their pupils, and in doing so, there were occasional implied criticisms about the quality of relationships between pupils and their teachers. Similar to comments about relationships there are often comments about TAs being on the same level as the pupils which may suggest that the social distance between teachers and pupils remains an issue in the eyes of some TAs.

Exercise 1.1   The advantages of being a TA

Look at the quotations below from TAs and other support staff about the pluses that they possess in dealing with behaviour difficulties and disruption. Tick the box of the three quotations that you identify with the most. There is a blank row at the end of the list for you to add any other advantage not included here.

Quotation	Tick
I am closer to the children and I think I am enabled to be more human in response and less authoritative.	
Having the time to communicate on a more personal level.	
You are able to spot potential problems before they get out of hand because you do not have to concentrate on delivering the lesson … and you are often sat with the students. You are then able to 'nip it in the bud' or distract or persuade.	
I can usually spot it and deal with it before it gets out of hand and becomes more disruptive.	
Being able to work with students on a 1:1 before the behaviour disrupts others.	
We are closer to the pupils and are not seen as an official, therefore we can get a greater understanding of the behaviour.	
Stronger relationships with students generally than teachers … working at ground level … more personal knowledge of students' lives.	
Relationship with student, know strategies that work and build up trust. In among the children, have a better perspective of what is going on.	
You get to work with students more to get to the root of the behaviour problem. I think then you can have a closer relationship with the student and know how to deal with behaviour better.	
A unique opportunity to interact with pupils and operate more on their level.	
I am free to deal with this behaviour while the teacher carries on with the lesson. I can deal individually with the pupils at a friendship level.	

The disadvantages of being a teaching assistant/ member of support staff

One of the major developments in schools in the last decade has been the changing role of the TA and the increasing employment of non-teaching staff of various descriptions undertaking key supportive roles in learning and teaching in schools (Townsend and Parker, 2009). The teacher is now much more defined as a manager of learning. In the best of practices it is difficult to distinguish which adult is performing which role and the classroom becomes a vibrant centre of learning where all are agreed on objectives, rules and ways of working. Every adult makes a contribution, knows what they are doing and feels valued.

When asked to consider the disadvantages of being support staff and TAs four broad groups emerge:

- low status;

- inconsistency in application of classroom and school rules;

- relationship tension;

- clashes of practices, beliefs and values.

Low status

The first disadvantage is based upon the status that TAs possess and the frustrations that accompany that status. Much of this can be countered by the manner in which TAs are supported by the school and also by the way that teachers and support staff work together as a team with uniform and shared objectives. Despite the advances in recruitment, training and role definition of TAs, in some schools they are still employed to undertake tasks that perpetuate a low-status role from which they find it hard to develop any authority in dealing with difficult pupil behaviour.

Inconsistency in application of classroom and school rules

A second disadvantage is inconsistency in the way that behaviour matters are dealt with between classes in which TAs are working or breaks in continuity which do not allow support staff to fulfil their full potential. Teamwork in classrooms (Pittman, 2009) is not automatic but has to be worked on and time needs to be given to agreeing what is important about a lesson, programme of study and ways of working to help to secure consistency and create a seamless classroom operation. This helps TAs to absorb some of the authority of their teacher colleagues in the context of a collaborative partnership.

Relationship tension

This disadvantage is linked to a role that many support staff are asked to fulfil which is based on working alongside and supporting individual pupils. Sometimes the demands they make can lead to stress and there are also tensions when an authority stance is required to deal negatively with a pupil who is well known to them and with whom a good, even close, relationship has developed. The disruption that they are coping with is not of their making – indeed may have nothing to do with them – and it could be the case the TA empathises with the pupil.

Clashes of practices, beliefs and values

The fourth disadvantage is one which resonates strongly with the underlying theme of this book. TAs sometimes report tension between their practices, beliefs and values and those of teachers. Such tensions do not just exist between TAs and teachers but between TAs and TAs and between teachers and their fellow teachers. However, when combined with the other perceived disadvantages, the satisfaction that TAs experience in the workplace can be severely limited.

Although the four disadvantages have been separated it is clear from discussions with TAs that there is considerable overlap between them. For example, tension between staff may be a consequence of low status or a clash of values.

 Exercise 1.2   The disadvantages of being a TA

Look at the quotations below from TAs and other support staff about the negatives that they possess in dealing with behaviour difficulties and disruption. Tick the box of the three quotations that you identify with the most. There is a blank row at the end of the list for you to add any other disadvantage not included here.

Quotation	Tick
Sometimes depending on your relationship with the students they may not take you seriously as a figure of authority when trying to deal with behaviour issues. This can often stem from how they see the teacher relating to you and whether they treat you as an equal.	
Sometimes you see other adults dealing with a situation badly and you don't have the authority to deal with it yourself.	
I am sometimes expected to pass the incident on to the teacher as the 'higher person in authority' and the information I have is diluted. I am also undervalued as a member of staff in some circumstances.	
Lack of respect from some children. Lack of respect from some teachers.	
As a TA you're not always taken as seriously as a teacher and students will ignore instructions from you and you can feel disrespected.	
Pupils regard TAs as having less status and not able to enforce rules and sanctions.	
Teachers have different ways of working. Inconsistency.	
Being split between several different classes therefore no continuity.	
You can miss out on 'the bigger picture' while dealing with behaviour. I have a child who can't cope with the full lesson. I remove him for the last 15 minutes each time to 'cool off'. I feel isolated from my class and teacher when this happens. I don't feel that I am supporting the other children or the teacher.	
Not always seen to be of use. Not always being there – continuity – moving between four classes.	
Sometimes a hard balance with discipline when you have strong relational skills with students.	
Can be tiring as so many students tell you stuff and want to talk.	
Having different beliefs in behaviour compared to the teacher.	
Stepping on the teacher's toes.	

(Continued)

(Continued)

Feeling uncomfortable about how some people deal with difficult behaviour.	
Conflict of interest.	
Having to follow through with sanctions you don't always agree with.	

Whatever the pluses and minuses of the role of support staff in schools there is one constant and that is change (Lee, 2009)! Gone are the days of the 'Mum's Army': the new roles that TAs now occupy reflect increased status, demands and professionalism all of which come from external forces such as legislation, school requirements and a growing belief that TAs represent good value, not only in terms of finance but also skills. It is easy to imagine that they will continue to increase in number and influence in schools and that schools that seek to give TAs responsibility matched with appropriate training, status and remuneration will reap enormous rewards.

Further reading

Derrington, C. and Groom, B. (2004) *A Team Approach to Behaviour Management: A Training Guide for SENCOs Working with Teaching Assistants.* London: Paul Chapman.
Kamen, T. (2003) *Teaching Assistant's Handbook.* Oxford: Hodder Arnold.

Websites

www.tda.gov.uk/support/hlta
www.tda.gov.uk/support/nos

References

Lee, C. (2009) 'Positive approaches to behaviour management', in M. Parker, C. Lee, S. Gunn et al., *A Toolkit for the Effective Teaching Assistant,* 2nd edn. London Sage.
Lee, C. (2009) 'Understanding change and being part of it', in M. Parker, C. Lee, S. Gunn et al., *A Toolkit for the Effective Teaching Assistant,* 2nd edn. London: Sage.
Pittman, M. (2009) 'Working together: collaborative and supportive partnerships', in M. Parker, C. Lee, S. Gunn et al., *A Toolkit for the Effective Teaching Assistant,* 2nd edn. London: Sage.
Townsend, M. and Parker, M. (2009) 'Changing schools, changing roles for teaching assistants', in M. Parker, C. Lee, S. Gunn et al., *A Toolkit for the Effective Teaching Assistant,* 2nd edn. London: Sage.

2

Preventing disruption and promoting positive behaviour

This chapter looks at the four main areas which help to ensure that disruption is kept to a minimum. The skills of support staff are reflected upon through a self-evaluation exercise before we go on to look at the value of teams in which the overwhelming majority of TAs exist. There follows a consideration of the context – the classroom – and how effective classroom practice avoids generating situations that can be problematic. Finally, there is chance to look at the pupils and how knowledge of them can prove useful in understanding and preventing disruption.

By the end of the chapter you will have considered and gained a better understanding of:

- your own skills;
- the teams to which you belong;
- the context in which you work, i.e. the school and the classroom;
- your knowledge of the pupils.

Preventing problems

As noted in the last chapter HLTA Standards (www.tda.gov.uk/support/hlta) make one direct reference to behaviour matters recommending that HLTAs should 'use effective strategies to promote positive behaviour' (HLTA Standard 26). The emphasis on being able to 'promote positive behaviour' suggests that through well organised lessons and being a good role model there is less likely to be negative behaviour. Good planning, interesting learning experiences and

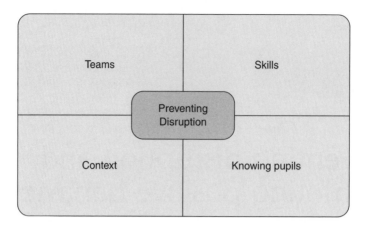

Figure 2.1   The prevention quadrant.

mutually respectful relationships will all help to ensure that the lesson runs smoothly and prevent disruptive behaviour. It is worth noting that there is no HLTA Standard which makes direct reference to TAs using their skills, influence and professional understanding to deal with low-level disruption and more extensive challenges to safety and order in the classroom. There is a requirement that TAs demonstrate that they 'recognise and respond appropriately to situations that challenge equality of opportunity' (HLTA Standard 27) which is a very important matter that merits its place in the list of Standards. Having said that, challenges to safety, order and relationships are frequent occurrences in the school day, indeed in individual lessons, and it is hard not to conclude that a phrase mentioning responding to challenging behaviour would improve Standard 26 so that it reads 'use effective strategies to promote positive behaviour and deal skilfully with disruptive and challenging behaviour'.

The title of this chapter refers to 'preventing' problems and, like 'promoting' positive behaviour there is no way of measuring how successful the lesson was and how much disruption was avoided, other than informal judgements such as 'that went well, no real problems' or 'that was far better than last time'. These kinds of judgements are important and invite follow-up questions such as 'how do I know it was far better than last time?' and 'what did I do that was better during this lesson?' Prevention is then hard to quantify, but requires considerable forethought and is supported by four key elements – the skills of the adult, whether teaching assistant or teacher, the context in which those skills operate, i.e. the classroom, effective class teams and knowledge of the pupils. All four contribute to minimising opportunities for disruption and a learning atmosphere (see Figure 2.1).

Skills

All effective classroom professionals develop the skill of making evaluative statements about their work and assessing their own skills. As a member of the support team in a school you start with practices which you know will help even if you have never worked in a school before – adapted parenting skills, things that you have heard are helpful or even ways that worked in your own school days and ways that you just think would work if a problem presented itself. Many of these skills derive from ways that you see as modelling good practice and effective behaviour management. Exercise 2.1 is list of characteristics, skills and attitudes that can help in both preventing and dealing with disruption – indeed many can help in both columns. They are among the ideals to which many TAs and other staff in schools aspire and most of them invite further comment that begins with 'because'. For example:

> 'I am able to remove a pupil if required to do so *because* I have been given this status and role by the class teacher and I possess the skills to do so' or

> 'I am consistent in the application of rules *because* I know them well and agree with what they are trying to achieve' or

> 'I have a positive attitude and a good sense of humour *because* they are good examples and convey an air of confidence to the pupils'.

Often the statements that occur after the 'because' in your answers will be those which show your status, experience, skills, values and principles – the last two of which will feature prominently in Chapter 3. It is important to make these statements because they help to celebrate your success, highlight areas that you might need to work on and identify which forms of approaches you find helpful and which could produce or reduce tensions for you.

The broad groups

Advice for TAs from the literature and relevant websites can be grouped into three key areas that overlap (see Figure 2.2).

Planning
Planning includes the learning experience, where appropriate, and anticipating potential behaviour problems. This does not mean guessing *who* will cause trouble and therefore considering how you will deal with them for the self-fulfilling prophecy could well operate and, because you anticipated problems, they occur. Avoidance of behaviour

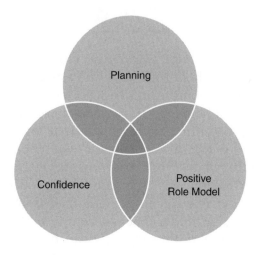

Figure 2.2   The skill triangle.

that is disruptive is more about *what* you will do and is a strategic way of thinking of what action will be required should certain behaviours happen, e.g. 'tactical ignoring' where if minor disruption occurs the initial reaction is not to respond knowing that attention to the problem will probably cause more disruption than the initial incident.

Confidence

Timidity, indecision and lack of self-belief in support staff are all predictable potential characteristics that create a vulnerability that some pupils might exploit but their opposites – dominance, inflexibility and arrogance – can also be problematic. Confidence is demonstrated by body language which is often said to convey a high percentage of what is really felt by a person. This is enhanced by possessing appropriate voice tone and volume, with a harsh tone and loud volume portraying a lack of care or an over-reliance on aggression. It is often the case that effective classroom practitioners have a quiet voice that commands attentive listening. Finally, assuming it is appropriate to your role, how you move around the classroom demonstrates responsiveness to any developing situation. Managing situations by proximity is a skill that can be learned, especially through knowledge of the pupils with whom you work. Should the tactical ignoring, mentioned in the previous section, fail then the next stage in the plan is often to move closer. When coupled with confident body language the situation can be dealt with without a word being spoken. There are times when proximity can be a threat and management at a distance is more likely to keep control, especially when tempers have been lost. The skill can be summed up as avoiding the temptation of being drawn into problematic situations by pupils but feeling able to move in when you are convinced that intervention will work.

Positive role model

A crucial way to avoid classroom problems is being a positive role model with demonstrations of respect, tolerance, patience, kindness and consideration for all. Your pupils know that you will listen to them and that you will be clear and consistent in your support and in the application of rules. Even when under pressure or clearly upset you remain calm and look to find solutions and whenever possible demonstrate a sense of humour but not at anyone else's cost. The positive/negative balance needs to be in favour of the former with extensive and wise use of praise and encouragement – more of this in the next chapter. Good work and good behaviour both need to be acknowledged and, where appropriate, rewarded and the TA should convey enthusiasm for the specific lesson and for learning in particular. Ironically part of being positive is to show awareness of personal strengths and weaknesses with a recognition that learning comes from making mistakes in new areas of knowledge and skills rather than being successful at things you can do already. Saying 'I did not handle that well, I'll try to do better next time' is about taking responsibility and being future orientated rather than dwelling on the mistake.

Observations from TAs

Observations of other members of the support team or teachers or perhaps our own experience as learners are often the starting point to an approach to behaviour management. One useful reflective way to think about good practice is from teaching assistants' own experience in schools – 'what worked *with* us will work *for* us'. When asked what kind of teacher or other adults they have come across during their own education or time as a TA who inspired or did not inspire learning, and when asked to consider what constituted good practice and what did not, the following positive characteristics of a good role model emerged:

- being consistent and fair with praise;

- being approachable;

- having a good sense of humour;

- being interesting and lively;

- being kind and caring;

- being a good listener;

- able to respond to a question and go off at a tangent yet return to the main objective;

- able to use story well;

- being calm, especially under pressure;

- having a passion for the subject or topic;

- smiling a lot and being cheerful;

- able to use practical tasks;

- possessing 'the look' when required;

- showing respect for individuals.

The negative sides of these characteristics identified by TAs are very much the opposite of the above list such as always shouting and ranting on and on, being too laid back, patronising, arrogant, smug, unapproachable, being critical of work and having a boring voice.

Assessing my skills

There are two Exercises (2.1 here and 3.1 in the next chapter) which form part of a process of reflective self-evaluation – you are appraising yourself. The skills selected are by no means the complete list and, although they have been divided into preventing and dealing with disruption, there is considerable overlap.

   Exercise 2.1   Assessing my skills

1. Consider each statement below that includes skills which help prevent disruption, deal with disruption and both. Rate your skills from 0 (I do not have this skill at all) to 10 (I possess this and could not improve upon it).

2. Select five for which you have given yourself the highest scores.

3. Write the statement on a piece of paper and add the reason for this celebration starting with 'because', e.g. 'I am consistent in the application of rules *because I know them well and agree with what they are trying to achieve'*.

4. At the end add any skill that you feel has been left out but which could contribute to the list.

Skill statement
My expectations are not too high nor too low
I ensure firm, clear, consistent and fair boundaries
I make sure pupils talk rather than shout
I have the ability to spot early signs of disruption
I am consistent in the application of rules
I know when I am getting emotionally involved and can control this
I am good mannered
I ensure I explain my expectations clearly
I know the pupils well and can name all those I work with
I have the ability to take control of a situation
I have a positive attitude and a good sense of humour
I am able to remove a pupil if required to do so
I am able to stay calm
I do not react badly to attention-seekers
I ignore minor behaviours
I ensure that pupils listen to me
I am a good role model and lead by example
I use plenty of praise and positive comments
I give clear, direct instructions
I am able to diffuse difficult situations
I possess good communication skills
I would add ...

Teams

The importance of teamwork cannot be emphasised enough in dealing with any form of disruptive behaviour. However many of the previously mentioned skills that support staff possess will be challenged or even negated, if they are working alongside a teacher who lacks the ability to manage the class and who, for example, often turns minor disruption into major conflict. The reverse also applies in that TAs who are not operating in harmony with successful classroom management practice and who possess the capacity to undermine the lesson and cause disruption rather than resolve it can destroy lessons. Talking about his research with two TAs and a class teacher Rix (2005) states 'each of them gives way to the other at different times out of respect for their role and because of their different abilities to work with pupils ... Rather than clearly designated boundaries between three individuals, theirs is a team endeavour.'

One way of analysing the level of teamwork is to look at the following adaptation of the criteria for effective teacher-TA teamwork from Vincett et al. (2005). Effective classroom teams will have:

1. *Senior manager involvement.* Senior managers with a clear vision for and commitment to classroom teamwork including non-contact time, time for meetings, professional development and review of performance.

2. *Self–recognition.* Classroom teams who value themselves, recognise the value of teamwork and acknowledge that teamwork skills can be enhanced.

3. *Established good practice.* All members of the team define: (a) effective practice, (b) common goals, (c) their roles in achieving (a) and (b). Such a model is crucial to achieving consistency in behaviour management.

4. *Common goals.* Agreed goals are not just about classroom work but also team processes. The team know what to deliver and are committed to its delivery.

5. *Communication and relationships.* Time that is given to planning and monitoring – to facilitate this TAs only work with a limited number of teachers and there is some joint professional development.

6. *Meetings*. Meetings that are planned and structured and views valued regardless of status, and they are fully costed, including pay and cover costs.

7. *Self-regulation*. Autonomous teams that are empowered to act independently and evaluate their progress against agreed targets.

8. *Celebration*. Frequent celebrations that are also celebrated by others.

As well as all the criteria set out above there is something about a good classroom team that means that they all look out for each other, they miss anyone who is absent, they celebrate each other's successes and they feel each other's pain. In discussions with TAs many reveal that they enjoy their jobs and feel fulfilled by their roles but some say that they do not always feel that they are part of a team. One of the many dilemmas they face is that their approaches to behaviour are often determined elsewhere. It may be the school behaviour policy which sets the climate for reaction to both positive and negative behaviours or it could be the class teacher who may have a specific regime that informs how difficult behaviour is managed. For example, some schools adopt certain clearly identified approaches to managing behaviour such as Assertive Discipline (Canter and Canter, 2001). Like any adult working in schools, TAs bring their own values and ideas to any situation and where these coincide with those of other adults or a specific scheme the result is consensus and teamwork; where they do not coincide one of the most likely outcomes is a frustrated and disenchanted workforce. All that has been set out in the models provided imply a team which consists of teacher and TAs but Pittman (2009) mentions the need for TAs to work with each other in a collaborative way. In the end whatever status, income and responsibility people possess they share two common features – they are the school staff and they are there to maximise the learning and security of the pupils.

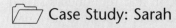 Case Study: Sarah

Among her many roles Katy supports pupils with special educational needs (SEN) in a small semi-rural secondary school. In some classes she finds she works with high numbers of pupils with additional needs as is the case of the Year 8 'Textiles' group. The

(Continued)

(Continued)

group, who have been making fleece hats, are mainly at the stitching together stage.

One Wednesday in the autumn term the group made their entrance in their usual noisy manner and because of some minor disruption they took a while to settle to the task. One of the pupils, Sarah, is among the most difficult of the pupils but has shown a recent improvement by not running out of the classroom at every opportunity. Katy focuses on Sarah's start and aims to ensure that she settles well. Katy has a fairly close relationship with Sarah who seems to respond well to her. However, lesson starts can be difficult because Sarah does not always mix well and some of her classmates irritate her and she has been known to disrupt them. Seating arrangements for this group are crucial to the success of the lesson. Karl, who has fallen behind with his work, decides that rather than aim to catch up, he will cause considerable trouble and irritate and distract others, resulting in his being sent out from the lesson. The atmosphere in the class has been affected by Karl's behaviour and the sending out.

Sarah is meant to be tacking the band onto her hat but continually keeps unthreading the needle as a way of getting Katy's attention. Given Katy's role is to support the pupils seen as having SEN in the group she is not always able to immediately respond and, when she fails on one occasion, Sarah seeks attention by saying that Liam is calling her names. Katy tries to buy some time by telling Sarah to ignore the name calling and that she will be with her soon. However, the denials from Liam lead others to say that he is calling her names and little work is being undertaken.

Eventually Sarah is helped to rethread the needle by Katy and she then attempts to help others which only leads to a further outbreak of arguing between Liam and Sarah. This time it is more aggressive and Laura leaves her seat and starts to kick out at Liam resulting in her being told that her behaviour is unacceptable by the teacher and she is the second pupil sent from the group. On her way from the classroom she states that Liam is bullying her and that leads to increased disruption and some pupils saying that the bullying accusation is true. There appears to be a pro-Liam and a pro-Sarah group and both pupils are attracting a lot of attention. To add further potential disruption Karl is invited to return to the class to continue with his hat but he feels he has fallen too far behind. He and a group of boys, appear to have spent most of the lesson achieving little and have been off target unless Katy or the teacher has been working directly with them.

Sarah's story raises many questions such as:

1. Is Katy's role, which is to focus on supporting the group of pupils with SEN, best served by her actions in this scenario?

2. Does the staff team appear to be working well?

3. Is sending pupils out of the room an efficient way of dealing with the disruption?

4. How could the teacher and Katy deal more effectively with two pupils who demand attention in a disruptive way?

Context

The term 'context' here applies to the classroom and other areas where group work takes place but much of what is said could be applied to the school as a whole. First there is the tangible part of the classroom, the room itself. The suitability of the desks or seats and their layout are important and just as significant here is the lighting, the temperature and the ambience which is enhanced by displays of pupils' work.

Second is the learning tasks that the pupils are asked to undertake, which need to be relevant, interesting and differentiated in accordance with pupil ability and methods of delivery. Despite the apparent rebelliousness of pupils who appear to be difficult to manage they, like most pupils, are conservative and enjoy routines such as timetables, teachers and TAs that rarely change. Lesson starts help to enforce the sense that learning is managed and it is crucial that the TA knows what their role is and what tasks they will be involved in or be managing. It cannot be emphasised enough that lesson starts that are clear, exciting, involving and well organised deter so many problems and, similarly, lesson endings round off the complete learning experience. All pupils, no matter what age, enjoy the learning experience when it is book-ended with clarity and efficiency.

Smith and Laslett (1993) suggested a four-rule model for teachers' classroom management that translates well for TAs, especially those who have a teaching role, but is also relevant for those who do not.

- *Rule 1*: **'Get them in'** places the emphasis on starting the learning experience, making sure pupils know what they will learn and what they need. A prompt start conveys a professional attitude and looks to involve pupils in the learning process as soon as possible.

- *Rule 2*: **'Get on with it'** requires lessons to have the right pace, content and tasks. Work is differentiated to accommodate varied needs and styles of learning and there are opportunities for cooperative learning and extension activities.

- *Rule 3*: **'Get on with them'** is about the importance of good working relationships with pupils and about being interested in them as individuals, being prepared to help them – in some cases it may need to be discreetly as not all pupils welcome help – and establishing routines for pupils to seek assistance. It is here that the teamwork that underpins effective professional practice comes to the fore and TAs often find themselves in the leading role.

- *Rule 4*: **'Get them out'** is not just about the exit from the classroom but about ensuring that there is time to restate the main lesson themes, tidy the room and leave in the orderly routine that all know. Saying 'goodbye' properly is the first part of saying 'hello' for the next lesson.

Finally, and perhaps more difficult to analyse than any other aspect of the context, is the respect that staff have for each other and their pupils, the role of support staff and the professional development of staff that leads to their capacity to intervene early in any potential situation that might lead to disruption. Just as it is good practice for the teacher to acknowledge the professionalism of the support staff in their lessons, so it also good practice for the TA to mention to the teacher when they feel it was a really good lesson. How often do classroom professionals fail to recognise and celebrate each other's skills? There is an often quoted piece of advice to 'catch them being good' which might also apply to adults. It boils down to respect *from* all involved *to* all involved and is probably best appreciated by the notion of the classroom atmosphere, which is so hard to define but you know it when you are in a good one!

Knowing pupils

The earlier list of personal attributes that help prevent problems is by no means a complete list and a deliberate omission is the pupil because the list is focused the skilled adult. Understanding the causes of a pupil's problems can help the TA to frame their response if a pupil is being disruptive and can help in understanding their behaviour. Knowing about causal factors can be important but can also lead to allowing them to influence too many judgements. Whatever the background to disruptive behaviour and however much it is understood by all, it may still be disturbing the learning of others and undermining what is going on in the lesson and therefore it has to be dealt with. Much has been written about the possible underlying causes of specific pupil misbehaviour in schools and through undertaking Exercise 2.2 you will have the opportunity to reflect on a pupil that you know.

 ### Exercise 2.2 Influences on the behaviour of a known pupil

Consider a child or young person who you are working or have worked with and about whom you feel that your knowledge of them has informed your dealings with them. In the notes section:

1. Tick the relevant cause or influences.

2. Write why this cause or influence is particularly important.

3. Consider the dangers or limitations of emphasising that cause or influence.

Cause or influence	Further information and examples	Notes
Family circumstances	Concern over parenting, siblings, parental break-ups, lifestyle at home, e.g. are they indulged with material goods as a substitute for attention and affection.	
Stage of development	Early years, adolescence or educational stage, e.g. transition.	
Notions of self	How pupils see themselves – and self-esteem – how they perceive the gap between their perceptions of self and their desired self may influence their behaviour and their achievement.	
Gender	The need sometimes for boys to demonstrate their 'macho-ness' and girls to feel secure in close relationships with a small group of peers.	

(Continued)

(Continued)

Emotional well-being at the time	How they are dealing with what is happening outside the classroom, maybe at home, social or non-classroom based elements such as playgrounds, journeying to and from school (e.g. bullying).	
Special educational need	Sometimes the pupil has a specific SEN which determines their behaviour, e.g. ADHD, and others have specific needs such as hearing impairments which may lead to frustration and consequent behaviour difficulties.	
Physical and mental health	Both are important in their own right as well as the relationship between the two of them.	
Immediate environment	The classroom environment, the prevailing weather and the number of pupils in the class.	
Culture	This is not always about, but includes, race and class culture.	

The issues are not as distinctive and separate as they are stated here and such an exercise renders a complex matter too simple. Many pupils experience what some might define as negative experience linked to the factors listed above and perhaps other factors but they do not exhibit behaviour difficulties; conversely, others pupils can appear to have high self-esteem, have seemingly excellent relationships with caring parents and are not going through a predictably difficult stage in their development yet still their behaviour is highly disruptive. It also raises fundamental questions for the TA about understanding pupil behaviour and their capacity to manage it. Whatever the level of knowledge about the above in relation to an individual pupil, will that knowledge help them prevent or deal with any difficulties? The answer is 'variable' – many of the items mentioned in Exercise 2.2 will determine our relationships with and reactions to pupils but others will have no impact at all. Fundamentally, skilled practitioners look more at their own values, ideas and skills than at the issues that influence the pupils. In the end it amounts to the answer to a single question – what do I have more control over: (1) the child's gender, their parenting experiences or the culture, which are, of course, significant issues that merit consideration; or

(2) my ability to create a learning environment and deal with any threats to that environment in the form of pupil behaviour?

Further reading

Chaplain, R. (2003) *Teaching Without Disruption in the Primary School: A Model for Managing Pupil Behaviour.* London: RoutledgeFalmer.

Charlton, T. and David, K. (1993) *Managing Misbehaviour in Schools.* London: Routledge.

Hill, F. and Parsons, L. (2000) *Teamwork in the Management of Emotional and Behavioural Difficulties.* London: David Fulton.

McNamara, S. and Moreton, G. (1995) *Changing Behaviour: Teaching Children with Emotional and Behavioural Difficulties in Primary and Secondary Classrooms.* London: David Fulton.

Riddall-Leech, S. (2003) *Managing Children's Behaviour.* Oxford: Heinemann.

Wearmouth, J. (1997) 'Pygmalion lives on', *Support for Learning,* 12 (3): 20–5.

Websites

www.tda.gov.uk/support/hlta

References

Canter, L. and Canter, M. (2001) *Assertive Discipline,* 2nd edn. Los Angeles: Canter Associates.

Pittman, M. (2009) 'Working together: collaborative and supportive partnerships', in M. Parker, C. Lee, S. Gunn et al., *A Toolkit for Effective Teaching Assistants,* 2nd edn. London: Sage.

Rix, J. (2005) 'A balance of power: observing a teaching assistant', in R. Hancock and J. Collins (eds), *Primary Teaching Assistants: Learners and Learning.* London: David Fulton.

Smith, C. and Laslett, R. (1993) *Effective Classroom Management: A Teacher's Guide.* London: Routledge.

Vincett, K., Cremin, H. and Thomas, G. (2005) *Teachers and Teaching Assistants: Working Together.* Maidenhead: Open University Press.

3

Intervention approaches

This chapter begins by focusing on dealing with disruptive behaviour and by the end of the chapter you will have a better understanding of your values and beliefs and how they might be categorised into three approaches to intervention. It begins with a self-assessment of your skills before an engagement with *your* values and *your* beliefs through a questionnaire based upon making choices about classroom scenarios and more general beliefs about pupils. The three approaches – system, negotiation and relationship – are briefly described prior to a case study of how one secondary school, the TAs in early years contexts and care staff in a special school responded to the questionnaire.

Values and beliefs

This chapter encourages you to build on the process of an in-depth self-assessment of your skills that you began in the previous chapter and moves on to look at the beliefs and values that support those skills. The starting point is a self-assessment involving an inventory which looks at the *values and beliefs* you hold and how these might relate to ways of working with pupils.

As an adult working in a school and classroom you bring your talents and skills to the role but, as stated before, you bring much more than that: you bring your values and beliefs. It is these that help to begin to inform ideas and skills on behaviour matters and how you will react when difficulties present themselves in the classroom. Belief systems are the generalisations that everyone makes about life and are the personal rules about ourselves and others and that include the behaviour of others and of ourselves. Gordon (1996: 11) describes the idea of self-fulfilling prophecy as 'powerful'. Adopting this approach then, the TAs who believe that they can succeed will be more likely to succeed and those who believe they cannot succeed may well not. These beliefs are linked to the confidence and self-esteem of the adults in the classroom. They are not the only beliefs that contribute to our reaction to disruption as there are also those which are linked to judgements we make about how behaviour should be interpreted and what we believe to be right. These more moral and ethical judgements we might call 'values'. An illustration of this is that many people are outraged by the bullying they see among their pupils and possess a broad definition of what constitutes bullying while others see it as part of growing up and only requiring intervention if it is persistent. The values we possess and the beliefs that we hold underpin what we see as disruptive, disturbing or challenging and what we are prepared to do about it.

The beliefs inventory

In order to help you begin a deeper engagement with your beliefs and how they relate to approaches to dealing with disruptive behaviour it is important to engage in reflection on what ideas you have about educational questions and how these relate to your principles and values. To set that process in motion Exercise 3.1 begins by asking you to focus on your thoughts about your beliefs and values. You then complete the inventory that has been adapted from the work of Glickmann and Tamashiro (1980) who have used a similar model to help other caring professionals examine their beliefs and ideas. The purpose of the inventory is for teaching assistants, cover supervisors and other support staff to assess their own beliefs on classroom discipline and control. It is based upon making *forced choices* in response to two given options for each question and then recording your choices on the accompanying, score sheet.

 Exercise 3.1 The beliefs inventory

Instructions

You are going to make twelve *forced choices* in response to two given options for each question. Select either answer A or answer B for each question. You may not completely agree with either choice but choose the

(Continued)

(Continued)

one that is closer to how you feel and think. In seven cases there is a scenario to which you respond by making one of the choices.

No.	Choices	A or B
1.	**A:** Although pupils think, the decisions they make are not fully rational and moral. **B:** Pupils' inner emotions and decision-making processes must always be considered legitimate and valid.	
2.	**A:** When teaching a group or class, generally I assign pupils to specific areas in the classroom. **B:** Generally, my seating arrangements are open to negotiation.	
3.	**A:** No matter how limited the pupils' opportunities may be, pupils should still be given the responsibility to choose and make decisions. **B:** Teaching assistants and other adults need to realise that, in addition to their effect on pupils during school hours, pupils are greatly influenced by their own families, the neighbourhoods where they live, their peers and television.	
4.	*When the high noise level in a group or classroom bothers me, I will be more likely to ...* **A:** Discuss my discomfort with the pupils and attempt to come to a compromise about noise levels during activity periods. **B:** Allow the activity to continue as long as the noise level is not disturbing or upsetting any pupil.	
5.	*If a pupil breaks a classmate's mobile phone that the pupil brought to school, I will be more likely to ...* **A:** Reprimand both children, one for disrespecting other people's property and the other for breaking a rule that prohibits bringing mobile phones to school. **B:** Avoid interfering in something that the pupil (and possibly their parents) needs to resolve themselves.	

6.	*If pupils unanimously agree that a classroom rule is unjust and should be removed but I disagree with them …* **A:** The rule should probably be removed and replaced by a rule made by the pupils. **B:** The pupils and I should jointly decide on a fair rule.	
7.	*When a pupil does not join in a group activity …* **A:** I should explain the value of the activity to the pupil and encourage them to participate. **B:** I should attempt to identify the child's reasons for not joining and should create opportunities that respond to those reasons.	
8.	*During the first week of a new year or with a new group I will more likely to …* **A:** Let the pupils interact freely and let them initiate any rule making. **B:** Announce the class rules and inform pupils how the rules will be fairly enforced.	
9.	**A:** A pupil's creativity and self-expression should be encouraged and nurtured as much as possible. **B:** Limits on destructive behaviours need to be set without denying pupils their sense of choice and decision.	
10.	*If a pupil interrupts the lesson by talking to a neighbour, I will be more likely to …* **A:** Move the first pupil away from the others and continue the lesson because time should not be wasted on account of one individual. **B:** Tell those pupils involved how angry I feel and conduct a dialogue about how the first pupil would feel if they were interrupted.	
11.	**A:** A good teaching assistant is firm but fair in taking disciplinary actions with the pupil who violates a school rule. **B:** A good teaching assistant discusses several alternative disciplinary actions with the pupil who violates a school rule.	

(Continued)

(Continued)

| 12. | When one of the more conscientious pupils does not complete a piece of work on time ...
A: I will assume the pupil has a legitimate reason and that the pupil will hand in the piece of work when he or she completes it.
B: I will tell the pupil that he or she was expected to hand in the piece of work when it was due and then, with the pupil, we will decide on the next steps. | |

Scoring
Circle your response on the following tables and add up the totals in each table.

Table 1		Table 2		Table 3	
2A	1A	2B	4A	4B	1B
3B	5A	3A	6B	6A	5B
7A	8B	7B	9B	9A	8A
11A	10A	11B	12B	12A	10B

Your beliefs

Total number of responses in Table 1: *The System Approach*
Total number of responses in Table 2: *The Negotiation Approach*
Total number of responses in Table 3: *The Relationship Approach*

All the major behaviour management techniques can be character-ised as a continuum with adult power and priorities at one end and pupil power and priorities at the other. The three categories 'System', 'Negotiation' and 'Relationship' have been described slightly differ-ently by Wolfgang (2005) who categorised intervention approaches in relation to the notion of the power of the teacher and used the continuum to construct three main groups described as:

- 'Rules and Consequences' (System);

- 'Confronting and Contracting' (Negotiation);

- 'Relationship and Listening' (Relationship).

The continuum is based upon the relative influences of adults' or pupils' issues on approaches with adults possessing high levels of power at the 'Rules and Consequences' end, more evenly balanced approaches in the middle under 'Confronting and Contracting' and pupil issues at the other end under 'Relationship and Listening'. All three are concerned with engaging with pupils with a view to dealing with disruption and providing support if required, and neither Wolfgang's terms nor the ones used in this book incorporate the most extreme reactions to disruption. They are, at one end, having no choice but to respond radically such as excluding a pupil for a serious assault or controlling their behaviour through medication and at the other end, allowing pupils total freedom to behave as they wish.

Until this book there was no equivalent continuum in existence for TAs and, given that the TA's role is not one that is based on the same status in the classroom as the teacher, their differentiated role needs to be taken into account. In the overview of this book the merits and problems of having the potential to draw upon multiple approaches was discussed and the ability and opportunity to call upon a variety of approaches is a positive feature of dealing with disruptive or challenging behaviour for all adults (Porter, 2000; Lee, 2007). However, given that support staff and TAs do not have the status and power that comes from the position of teacher the three categories have been adapted for the more ancillary role, hence 'System', 'Negotiation' and 'Relationship'. Through their role the TA is uniquely placed to move along this continuum and use a variety of skills and approaches to resolve any difficulty. To do this to their full potential they need to be aware of the breadth of approaches, hence this book, and also possess the support and understanding of other adults within the school. They also need to be aware of the possible problems that occur when they are involved in a difficult situation that is dealt with in a way which clashes with their beliefs and values.

To help to define the three areas it is important to consider the power relationship with the pupil and the fundamental assumptions behind the approaches.

The system approach

The school system is expressed through policies, values, structures, rules, rewards and sanctions that help to create order and an effective school climate. The system helps all those who work in the school to achieve common goals and bases itself on common practices which may be agreed by the personnel in the school or dictated to them.

Assumptions

- Pupils are required to behave well because order and discipline are key components for the learning environment.

- Pupils are being prepared for a society which embraces rules as part of a system of law and order and for work, where compliance and obedience are likely to be demanded.

- Children are capable of misbehaviour if they are not restrained by adults.

- Adults possess power over pupils and they use that power supportively to secure order for the classroom or the school.

Power

In some cases adults possess considerable power over pupils and they use that power supportively to secure order for the classroom or the school. TAs increasingly form a key part of the system although they do not automatically have the same power and status as their teacher colleagues. For TAs to be seen initially as powerful forces they may need to be supported by teachers who openly ensure that their authority is extended to the TA. Of course, this presupposes that they possess such power and authority themselves.

It is important to state here that this approach should not be confused with the 'Systemic', sometimes referred to as the 'Ecosystemic', approach developed by Molnar and Lindquist (1990) which focuses on the perception of behaviour and the complexity of influences on and interpretations of that behaviour. The system in the context of *this* book refers to the structure and organisation of the school itself and all that emerges from it such as policies and staff organisation.

The negotiation approach

The role of the TA is to provide pupils with the opportunity to make choices and understand the decisions they make and the consequences of those decisions. In negotiating with the pupil the TA will provide a balance between the needs of the pupil and those of others in the classroom including the adults.

Assumptions

- Preparation for a role in democratic society underpins this approach and pupils need to be taught the social skills that allow them to take their place in a democracy. Included in these are negotiation skills and the ability to resolve conflicts and/or differences.

- Children, who are inherently good, need a supportive environment to help their social skills to develop.

- More responsibility and power rests with the pupil and negotiations with them need to be undertaken with a view to ensuring understanding that their behaviour must change but that their needs can still be met.

Power

The idea here is to place more responsibility and power with the pupil, and to negotiate with them with a view to ensuring understanding that their behaviour must change and comply. Emphasis is placed on helping pupils to understand the consequences of their actions, in a supportive and not authoritarian manner, and how their needs might still be met and the impact that their behaviour has on others.

The relationship approach

The TA offers support and clarification that helps the pupil deal with the situation for themselves. The pupil is empowered to make choices and take ownership of the situation wherever possible. It is a more therapeutic notion of managing classroom difficulties and the TA makes use of high levels of interpersonal skills in a supportive manner which requires a mutually trusting relationship.

Assumptions

- Children have the capacity to fulfil their potential if they are given choices and the necessary freedom to seek their own ends. They may need support in the achievement of those ends.

- Personal fulfilment is linked to their freedom as children who are again considered to be inherently good.

- The TA provides support that helps the pupil to feel empowered and supports the pupil in meeting their needs.

Power

In this case the agenda is owned by pupils and adults, and the TA offers support and clarification that helps the pupil deal with the situation. Change in behaviour is determined by the pupil but with support coming from the TA and reflects on the more therapeutic notion of managing classroom difficulties.

No matter what the approach favoured or the one adopted – they are not always the same thing – a significant principle of effective behaviour management is establishing control over that which can definitely be controlled. Like their teacher colleagues, indeed even more than them, TAs need to ask a key question. 'What is it that I really have *control* over with this child, group or class?' The answer to this, of course, is very little. However, adults in a classroom do have control over one thing – themselves. This includes the creation of the learning environment, the organisation of the class or group and their response to any disruption. All too often behaviour is about the pupil and their problems and too little is said about the behaviour of the adults. This book looks at both but there is no doubting that the focus is on the latter. In a similar vein the key question could be. 'What *power* do I have in this school or class-room?' The answer here may well be 'very little' but change the central term from 'power' to 'influence' and the answer could be very different. TAs possess a great deal of influence on what happens in a classroom and many have a profound influence on the development of the pupils with whom they work. Exercise 3.2 invites you to begin to distinguish between important terms such as 'correct', 'influence' and 'forces'.

Exercise 3.2   The difference that TAs make

For each question list five answers. Then in the spaces provided (labelled Questions 1, 2 and 3) answer the following questions:

1. Which was the easiest question to answer?

2. Which of the three terms ('control', 'power' or 'influence') do you feel best represents your position in your professional role?

3. Which term do you prefer? Explain why you chose it.

Question	Your response
What control do I have in the classroom?	1. 2. 3. 4. 5.
What power do I have in the classroom?	1. 2. 3. 4. 5.
What influence do I have in the classroom?	1. 2. 3. 4. 5.
Question 1	
Question 2	
Question 3	

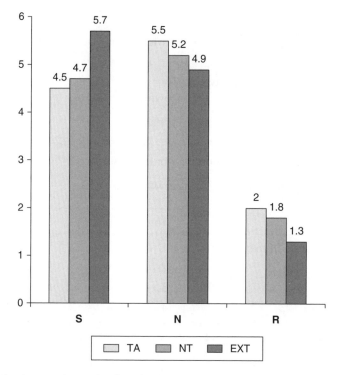

Figure 3.1   A secondary school and the three approaches.

The inventory in practice

As part of the research for this book staff from a small/medium size comprehensive school were invited to complete a version of the inventory which was very similar to the one used in this book. The major difference was that instead of 'TA' the term 'staff' was used. In all 43 staff took part and they were divided into three categories:

1. Teaching assistants and support staff 'TA' – 14 in total;

2. New teachers 'NT' ('new' being defined as in their first three years as a teacher) – 11 in total;

3. Experienced teachers 'EXT' – 18 in total.

The results of who saw themselves as being 'System', 'Negotiation' or 'Relationship' based are shown in Figure 3.1.

Analysis of the results provided some differences in their beliefs about discipline. The sample is too small to be considered valid in research terms so what is offered here must be regarded as tentative but of interest. The lowest score for the first column, i.e. those whose beliefs are located in the value of the system, came from the TAs and the highest from experienced staff. In contrast TAs appeared to be the group that saw the role of negotiating and contracting with pupils as more significant. All groups placed less value on the relationship aspect, although it was the TA group that appeared the highest. From this exercise more questions than answers emerge and these include:

1. Do experienced teachers become dependent on the system to enforce discipline and create the prevailing climate in school? They seem to see their relationships with pupils and how this relates to discipline as less important. Perhaps class sizes, concerns about safeguarding issues and relative ease of resorting to the system for support have not helped to nurture a relationship-based culture.

2. Do TAs find themselves more involved with individual pupils and therefore more inclined to emphasise the negotiated nature of discipline? They are probably the group who have more need of the system for support, certainly more than experienced teachers.

3. Do our beliefs change depending on the type of school and the role we play, or could it be that we choose to undertake a role that suits our beliefs?

4. Given that they require elaborate systems in order to function, do secondary schools place less emphasis on the relationship aspect of discipline than primary schools?

The most poignant moment that occurred during the discussion that followed the completion of the inventory that produced the chart in Figure 3.1 came from a member of the experienced teacher group, indeed a member of the senior management team, who openly stated that 'I am acutely aware that I should be placing more emphasis on relationships than the system. I feel that I simply do not have the time for this that I should have.' What this comment indicated was how frustrating it is when the beliefs about your practice may not match deeper held beliefs about the nature of the work you should be doing.

Returning to the list of questions above perhaps TAs in primary education would produce different results from their secondary colleagues. Following completion of the questionnaire by 46 TAs at a conference who work in either the early years or primary

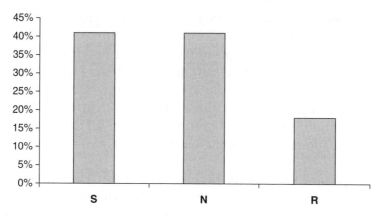

Figure 3.2   Early years and primary TAs.

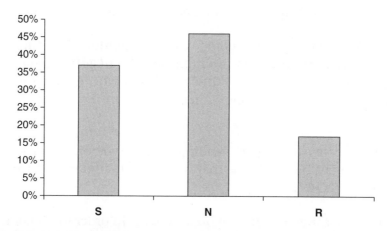

Figure 3.3   Special school.

sectors, the results suggest there is little difference between their views and those of their secondary colleagues. Forty-one per cent of responses favoured the system, the same percentage favoured negotiation and 18 per cent selected the relationship answers (see Figure 3.2).

In search of potentially different answers, the inventory was completed by care staff – the vast majority of whom work with young people with extensive behaviour difficulties and some of whom also exhibit quite substantial difficulties with learning. Even with a relatively small sample, just 23 staff, the results showed very little difference (see Figure 3.3).

The three approaches: opportunity or threat?

The three broad ways of dealing with disruption mentioned earlier, 'System', 'Negotiation' or 'Relationship', are usually suited to certain approaches that are in turn underpinned by what is and what is not valued by the classroom practitioner. However, very few TAs, support staff or, for that matter, teachers find they operate solely in one category. Much depends on the type of incident, the pupils involved and the broader context. Having a range of approaches is important and advantageous for any classroom practitioner, especially one who does not carry the authority that is attached to a title such as 'teacher', 'head of department' or 'deputy head teacher'.

Against all the positive elements of the three approaches two significant issues are raised: first, not all staff are comfortable with *all* of the approaches, and, second, not all staff are able to make use of them. Consider the following:

- The teacher who teaches eight different subject classes a day in a busy secondary school: there may be few opportunities to build rapport and relationships with individual pupils. To their credit many manage this against all the odds.

- The TA working with challenging Year 8 or 9 classes who is not familiar with all the school's rules, has had no say in their development and, as a result of their role and status, lacks traditional authority as a means of enforcing rules or applying sanctions: what significance is the seemingly remote 'system' for them?

- Staff working in early years settings where the pupils are just beginning their life in school and require order yet without having that order imposed in an authoritarian way but rather in a way that nurtures a climate of mutual respect.

It is hard to imagine that TAs and teachers do not approach their professional duties without possessing values and principles that underpin all their work. Often circumstances compromise these resulting in stress, and feelings of frustration and a lack of coherence and teamwork become distinct possibilities. Not everyone feels comfortable operating under all three approaches, despite it being highly likely they will be required to do so and opportunities will present themselves that call upon a variety of skills and ways of looking at the problem. Yet it is important that values and beliefs are made explicit so that, even where there are different opinions between the adults in the team, this may have a positive effect. Although easily seen as a disadvantage, differing roles and skills do not have to be negative, they can be an opportunity to bring a breadth of complementary skills to the complex classroom world.

The major issues would then appear to be:

- What are the values held by adults?

- How do they impact on practice?

- What do they mean for the ways that difficult behaviour is handled?

Whatever the outcome of completing the inventory in Exercise 3.1 it is important to recognise that in different circumstances there may be some changes in the answers given as our beliefs can change with time, status and context. Moreover, there are only twelve forced choices so it offers little more than a guide to your belief sets. Nonetheless, the inventory serves to prompt discussion, affirm opinion and differentiate between the three approaches to which the focus of this book now turns.

Further reading

Ayers, H. and Gray, F. (1998) *Classroom Management: A Practical Approach for Primary and Secondary Teachers.* London: David Fulton.

Ayers, H., Clarke, D. and Murray, A. (1995) *Perspectives on Behaviour: A Practical Guide to Effective Interventions for Teachers.* London: David Fulton.

References

Gordon, G. (1996) *Managing Challenging Children.* Nuneaton: Prim Ed Publishing.

Glickman, C. and Tamashiro, R. (1980) 'Determining one's beliefs regarding teacher supervision', *NASSP Bulletin,* 64: 74–81.

Lee, C. (2007) *Resolving Behaviour Problems in Your School.* London: Paul Chapman Publishing.

Molnar, A. and Lindquist, B. (1990) *Changing Problem Behaviour in Schools.* San Francisco: Jossey-Bass.

Porter, L. (2000) *Behaviour in Schools: Theory and Practice for Teachers.* Maidenhead: Open University Press.

Wolfgang, C. (2005) *Solving Discipline and Classroom Management Problems: Methods and Models for Today's Teachers,* 6th edn. Hoboken, NJ: John Wiley.

The system approach

> This chapter focuses on the school and the system that it provides to maintain order and support the agreed standards of behaviour. By the end of the chapter you will have considered and gained a better understanding of:
>
> - what is meant by 'system' in this context;
> - the positive side of what the system seeks to achieve;
> - the negative side of what the system seeks to achieve.
>
> Here the needs of the whole school population are the most significant and their values are represented by the school system. After a self-assessment of school policies, the remainder of the chapter looks at the positive system that schools put into place through rules and rewards, followed by the negative system that considers punishment and sanctions, before considering the value of adopting a consequence-based approach.

Even the smallest of schools have systems and procedures that aim to secure consistency: they use policy, rules, rewards and sanctions to that end. These say much about what might best be termed the 'climate' of the school as they ensure compliance and order through authority. 'Authority' is a term that can have many meanings and can have a negative interpretation. One meaning in the school context could be 'we (the senior staff) have constructed these rules, rewards and sanctions linked to our policies and the pupils must comply with them without question, as we know best!' Alternatively, it could be seen as 'we have listened to all parties and involved as many of them as possible in the construction of our rules, rewards and sanctions, and they now help to set the standards for school which we will all endeavour to achieve'. Authority in the latter statement is designed as a more democratic framework that secures compliance and involvement, and is not simply a remote statement from figures in authority. Whatever form authority takes, it has one major positive feature for TAs and support staff. It allows the system to take much of the pressure and, in giving rewards or applying sanctions, you are representing the system. In the application and enforcement of rules or sanctions it means that you are able to use the system to moderate any negative response, and it depersonalises enforcement to some degree. All you are doing is applying decisions made elsewhere and which all others have to comply with. Unfortunately, in the heat of the application of a sanction, the pupil may not see the democratic nature of the system and anger tends to be directed at people rather than seemingly remote systems. Enforcing systems, especially those where decisions have been made by people who may be remote from the daily management of pupils, is not without stresses and those stresses become exacerbated if you are not in agreement with the values being promoted. Hence, the merit of making values explicit and being clear about values is a major principle behind this book.

What will be crucial to the way the TA deals effectively with disruptive behaviour is their understanding of the main features of the system. These include:

- the main school policies;

- the mission statement (or similar overarching statement of principles);

- the school rules and how they are agreed and enforced;

- the reward system and how it is applied;

- the sanction system and how it operates.

Not only does a TA need to know these and what the implications are but, for them to be effective, they also need to be given sufficient status and back-up to enforce them when required to do so. Ultimately this will involve professional development and training which lead to deepened *knowledge* for new TAs arriving in the school and, even better, the *involvement* of members of the support team in the generation of component parts of the system. If TAs are not valued sufficiently and not invited into the full staff team then they will not be able to explore their system role effectively. It is hard to imagine that a TA who has been involved in creating policy will not have knowledge of it but, in this context, knowledge is more than knowing. It is about understanding why things are done and what are the most effective practices. In addition, many support staff are involved in single aspects of system development but not necessarily the 'bigger picture' components such as whole school policies.

Exercises 4.1 and 4.2 are not designed to offer a perfect description of how TAs are seen in your school. As a member of the support staff you may be content to be involved minimally and concentrate on the job of working with an individual pupil but what the exercises aim to do is make you reflect on your position and consider whether you are developing as a full member of the staff team. The central argument here is that TAs who have been given a role and some responsibility that demands dealing with behaviour matters benefit from being fully involved in the school and fully aware of key developments in the system.

 Exercise 4.1   Evaluation of the system

Consider the five components of the school system and rate your knowledge in the middle column from 0 (I do not know about this at all) to 10 (I know this very well indeed).

Consider your involvement in the five components and rate your involvement in them in the middle column from 0 (I have not been involved in this at all) to 10 (I was closely involved in this). Add up your score in each column and move on to Exercise 4.2.

School system components	Knowledge (rating 1–10)	Involvement (rating 1–10)
Main school policies, e.g. behaviour policy, SEN policy		
Mission statement or overarching statement of principles		

(Continued)

(Continued)

School rules and how they are agreed and enforced		
Reward system and how it is applied		
Sanction system and how it operates		
Total score		

 Exercise 4.2　Quadrant analysis

In Exercise 4.1, if your scores were under 25 in the 'Knowledge' column then, for the purposes of this exercise, you must consider yourself 'Low knowledge' and, similarly, if you scored under 25 for the 'Involvement' column then consider yourself as 'Low involvement'. If you have a score of 25 or above for either and you can consider yourself 'High knowledge' or 'High involvement'. Now plot your analysis of yourself in one of the quadrants below.

1. Does this seem a fair reflection of how you are seen?

2. Does this seem a fair reflection of how you see yourself?

3. If you are 'Low involvement' or 'Low knowledge' what would you like to see happen to increase either of them?

	High involvement	**Low involvement**
High knowledge	*High involvement/high knowledge* It is likely that you are playing a key role in your school or college. You have high status and the role that you play as a TA or member of support staff is valued.	*Low involvement/high knowledge* It is not likely that you are playing a fully developed role in your school or college. You may not have high status and the role that you play as a TA or member of support staff is not valued as fully as it might be.

	You have been involved sufficiently and/or received training that ensures your views are heard and respected. You are a key part of the school system.	You have been involved sufficiently and/or received training that ensures your skills are fully developed. You are sufficiently important to be kept informed and trained.
Low knowledge	*High involvement/low knowledge* It is not likely that you are playing a fully developed role in your school or college. You have quite high status but you have not been involved sufficiently and/or received training that ensures your skills are fully developed. You are important enough to be kept involved.	*Low involvement/low knowledge* It is likely that you are not playing a key role in your school or college. You would appear not to have high status and the role that you play as a TA or member of support staff is not valued as fully as it might be. You have not been involved sufficiently and/or received training that ensures your skills are fully developed. You are not a key part of the school in terms of involvement, knowledge and training.

Although there is no doubt that there has been an increase in the status of TAs and their training that has come a long way in recent times, schools have variable practice in how they use support staff. The most common forms of deployment are the general classroom ancillary, providing support with learning and the delivery of the curriculum and working with specific pupils deemed to have special needs. The latter role is a product of the system in which funding follows the pupil and helps to pay the salary of the supporting adult. In Chapter 1 there are quotations from some TAs who feel that they are too restricted and are 'not able to see the big picture', and they reflect on how their relationship with the teacher and their inter-changes impact upon their ability to deal with disruption. However, many contemporary schools are moving beyond these two models and are deploying support staff in a variety of imaginative ways, many of which are linked to closer roles in the behaviour management policy and also increasing involvement in delivery of the curriculum. The demography also appears to be changing in terms of who decides to be a TA with increasing numbers of young people becoming involved as well as teachers who want to move away from what they see as the bureaucracy attached to that role. Add to this the increased training opportunities through HLTA and Foundation Degrees and the simple models of old have been replaced by more complex scenarios, all of which demand creative ways of maximising the potential in classroom and school teams.

The positive system

Rules

The most obvious manifestation of the ideas set out in the policies, particularly the behaviour policy, should be the rules which underpin those policies and set the tone or climate of the school. They are expressions of the values held dear by those who created them and what the school deems to be good and what is desirable or undesirable. They have other functions too, in that they are an articulation of the unity of the school and create an opportunity for pupils to become involved in determining what is and what is not acceptable. And, of course, parents expect a school to have rules. Rules help pupils in their early years at school, pupils who may have experienced differing upbringings and notions of authority, to experience a single set of rules and a uniform school climate, and they help to teach pupils that without rules it is hard for a society to function properly.

One additional and highly significant function is that they help to support TAs in understanding their role in the system, and how they might use it when dealing with behaviour matters. The rule is helpful as it provides a focus for the TA to remind the pupil that they are beginning to be disruptive, such as 'Jack, remember the walking in class rule' which means stop running in class but is expressed in a more emotionally neutral manner. However, it is important that when enforcing the rule and when applying any sanction, the TA tries to emphasise that the sanction is not for *breaking the rule* but it is because what led to the rule being created has been violated and the rule needs to be used as a *reminder of the desirable behaviour*. For example, being asked to pick up litter as a sanction means little if it is no more than breaking the 'clean classroom rule', but it has significance if why the classroom needs to be litter free is understood together with the social and environmental implications of a dirty classroom. In addition, note that it is not expressed in a negative way, e.g. 'the 'no litter rule', but in the more positive 'clean classroom rule' which states the required outcome.

Consistency in the application of rules helps to ensure that they have meaning for the pupils and, in both tone and content, they need to be linked directly to approaches, rewards and sanctions. Therefore all TAs need to know what the rules are, and what their status is in the application of them. Wright (2005) makes a helpful distinction between *rules*, which are applied to all, and *directions*, which can vary in certain subjects or contexts. A science laboratory will require specific directions with regard to health and safety, and a TA working with young pupils with hearing or visual impairments may need additional rules related to such issues as noise and seating. Ideally TAs need to be involved in aspects of classroom regulatory systems including:

- talking: when it is permitted and when it is not;

- movement around the classroom;

- organising and presenting work;

- equipment/materials and how they must be used;

- social behaviour;

- safety;

- clothing: both uniform and for specialist tasks;

- space, including when the pupils need to be in the classroom.

Other good practice in the development and application of rules include the following:

- Ensure that they are expressed in language that can be understood or explained, especially in the case of young children and those pupils transferring from primary to secondary school.

- They do not change other than through a full-scale review. It is frustrating for all, but especially support staff, who find themselves enforcers of rules, if the rules have been changed but you have not been informed. It is good practice for TAs to occasionally ask those who coordinate their work about any potential adaptations or changes in rules.

- Keep them brief. With young children give the rule a verbal name, e.g. the 'walking rule' or the 'helping rule'.

- Keep the number of rules down to between four and eight which invite being memorised and ensure that they do not contradict each other.

- They should be clearly displayed as this permits easy enforcement through reference to the rule. Sometimes simply pointing to the rule sheet will do as a rule remainder.

- Rules gain in credibility when they are observable and seen as desirable as part of a genuine *whole* school approach and are applicable to both staff and students.

 ## Case study: Two schools

Often the rules themselves will mean little without enforcement and this notion applies to all forms of rules. They mean little, maybe nothing, if they are not enforced. Consider how these two secondary schools apply their rules on school uniform – an area which can generate considerable behaviour problems in their manifestation and enforcement.

School A

This medium-sized secondary school has enjoyed increasing success academically and is moving ahead on a number of fronts following the appointment of a new principal. Especially welcoming is the 'front of house' which has a friendly reception area that celebrates recent achievements of the school and its pupils. The centrepiece of the display area in the reception is the school uniform. There are information sheets, lists of suppliers and examples of the uniform itself – all in all it is a very impressive display, leading to the conclusion that the uniform is a key feature of the school. However, in the application of the rules there are problems and the most obvious example is the school tie. It must be worn by all pupils but for almost all of them what that appears to mean is worn with the knot 'at half mast' as one TA described it. Occasional reminders from staff are not proving successful because the uniform has been a source of contention among teaching staff. What has not been consistent is the backing of staff and the application of the rule. TAs are told that they, like their teaching colleagues, must enforce the rule on uniform but they find themselves in conflict with pupils and a few staff when they do so.

School B

This slightly larger school lacks the display at the hub of its entrance hall but, like School A, has made a commitment to school uniform. The uniform has been agreed in consultation between pupils, staff, governors and parent groups and is an expression of that agreement. New parents are informed of the rule regarding the wearing of school uniform and are not only told what it is but that it will be enforced and the school will look to them for support. The tie is worn in the conventional way, and although some pupils remove it when well away from school premises, there is almost total compliance in school. The TAs are told of the rules and told they will receive total backing from the senior managers if, in enforcing the rule, they are not treated with respect. All they usually find themselves having to do is a simple 'rule reminder'. The principal herself can often be seen discussing uniform issues with pupils including a high proportion of positive comments to pupils who are supporting the rule. Pupils get noticed for compliance and – very occasionally – non-compliance. It works well because the consultation phase was rigorous, there is backing for the rule, it is enforced and rules are taken very seriously in this school.

Whatever your views on school uniform, indeed on school ties, if it is part of the agreed set of rules then it needs to be taken seriously and complied with by all. Denial of one part of the rule can have the effect of undermining all rules and the TA's task becomes increasingly difficult, if not impossible. In the case of School A there are more problematic incidents related to uniform than in School B. Although the issue is the same, school uniform, the problems arise from how the rule was set up and the manner of the enforcement. Whatever the rule is and however it was arrived at, when it comes to enforcement it will not be just the rule that determines whether you are successful. It is more likely to be your tone of voice, body language and calm demeanour which generate an expectation of compliance and therefore you get it! Here the system combines with the individual's skills which cross into the two other broad approaches discussed in other chapters.

For those working in early years settings Wheeler (1996) noted that her pupils, aged between four and seven years, could produce lists of what she called 'acceptable behaviours', not rules. Her pupils produced a code of conduct in which each statement had an opening verb and then the reason for it, thus: 'Walking in class – is safer for everyone' and 'Talking nicely to each other – helps us make friends'. This approach provides an easily memorised verb plus the supportive purpose behind the rule. Wheeler also mentions how pupils were encouraged to identify and celebrate positive behaviour in others, and how important pupil participation and ownership of rules is to any whole-school approach and the alternative non-involvement of pupils makes the rules reflect an authoritarian, imposed model. It is important here to consider that if pupils are to be involved in rule construction, perhaps all those who will enforce them should be involved as well. Although the above was primarily aimed at early years practice the Key Stage 3 Strategy (DfES, 2004) suggests important features of rules that are similar and these are adapted slightly and included alongside other ideas in Exercise 4.3.

 ## Exercise 4.3   The important features of rules

There are many features of effective rule development and enforcement. Consider the list below and respond to each question.

1. Developed with pupils
2. Seen as fair by adults
3. Seen as fair by pupils
4. Few in number
5. Simple and clear
6. Understood by pupils
7. Stated as positive, required outcomes
8. Enforceable
9. Pupils understand the consequences of breaking the rules
10. Clearly displayed
11. Expressed in inclusive language
12. Applied consistently
13. Reflect the values (e.g. religion and lifestyle) of the community
14. Evaluated, reviewed and changed as necessary

Which three of the above are in your opinion:

1. The most important features?
   (a)
   (b)
   (c)
2. The ones that your school is best at ensuring?
   (a)
   (b)
   (c)
3. The ones that your school could improve upon?
   (a)
   (b)
   (c)

Rewards

When discussing the use of rewards in their schools TAs revealed their concerns that rewards were either the preservation of the brightest pupils or those who often behaved badly but were caught being good. Those pupils who worked fairly hard and were quiet and supportive did not appear to be rewarded as often. If true then this is illustrative of a poor functioning of the system. Rewards are being used to motivate the already motivated or bribe short-term changes in behaviour of the disruptive or antisocial. What is required is a reward system that is differentiated and allows all to have access. The other major danger is that pupils comply with a request or do not disrupt others because of the extrinsic motivation of the reward, not because they want to behave or see the purpose in it. There are occasions when tired members of staff will settle for this – just as long as they behave! However, conforming to the requirements of the system in order to gain a reward does not constitute effective practice and runs counter to the idea of 'consequences' which are discussed later in this chapter.

There are four basic types of reward:

- *social* rewards: celebrations through assemblies, letters to parents notices on boards;

- *object* rewards: badges, token and stars;

- *privilege* rewards: additional computer time, more choice or free time;

- *informal* rewards: including the relationship outcomes of being good to work with or kind to others.

While the first three rewards are usually part of either a class-based approach or a whole-school approach and, therefore, in the context of this book, are part of the system, the fourth is something deeper and harder to define. Often the close relationships between TAs and pupils are valued by both parties and it is an initial greeting at the beginning of the day, an acknowledgement throughout it or just an occasional smile that can matter more than tokens or material goods. As one special school stated in its policy. 'The most effective and enduring rewards that we are able to provide are our attention, affirmation and approval.'

Returning to the subject of more tangible rewards, they have been the subject of debate and some writers and teachers see them as little more than bribes, as ways of doing things *to* students not working *with* them (Kohn, 2001). Yet rewards, in all their forms, continue to be used and, as anyone who has picked up an education supplies catalogue will testify, there is an industry built around them. There is no doubt that rewards based on the observable or tokens are useful with younger pupils, and TAs working in these age groups note how their pupils enjoy rewards and how they provide a motivation, especially for those in school who struggle both with work and behaviour. However, they become somewhat redundant in the middle to late phase of secondary education, where the accusation of bribery could be even stronger. It would certainly not be seen as 'cool' for a 14-year-old to be singled out in assembly for good work or behaviour, and there is also the danger that they convey a model of interaction that is based upon a token system and not a strong supportive relationship. In addition, they can even foster a negative competitive ethos and pupils become rivals and even aggressive towards each other. The system rewards winners, which also means there will be losers, which can be demotivating.

Nonetheless, reward systems have much to offer schools especially if:

- they are linked to policies and rules help to define the expectations of the system;

- the construction of the reward systems is as open and as democratic as possible, which would mean including support staff in aspects of creating and application of rewards;

- it is accepted that there will be those who choose to remain outside the system but that they should not deliberately undermine it (any system, or part of it, is more likely to work if there is commitment to it and limitations and reservations have been shared among those involved);

The negative system

Working with TAs has revealed that the forms of negative behaviour they find most irritating are often the more constant interruptions experienced in many lessons and playgrounds. 'Rudeness', 'talking out of turn' ('tooting') and 'bad language' feature high on their lists. In keeping with public opinion both within and outside school, they feel that the behaviour of pupils in contemporary schools is becoming more antisocial and disruptive. They also convey that they do not have the power to deliver sanctions in the way that teachers can, and that either to use more subtle ways or to use none at all become the only options. Within the school behaviour policy and the system that supports it, there should be opportunities for TAs to utilise the system to enhance their capacity to apply sanctions if needed. Three preconditions must first be met for effective practice in this area. First, TAs need to know what authority they carry. Second, they should know more about sanctions deployed in their school and what appears to be effective for them and what is not effective or permitted. Finally, they should possess knowledge of what the options and outcomes are relating to these sanctions.

So far throughout this book the term most often employed to describe actions taken by staff because pupils have been disruptive has been 'sanctions'. However, there are other terms – many schools talk about punishments and others, perhaps the more enlightened, talk of 'consequences'. While the three terms are invariably used interchangeably, there are distinguishing features that have implications for TAs and support staff. Whichever one the TA uses depends on a number of factors, some of which you have control over and others which they are compelled to comply with. The choice made will be dependent upon:

- decisions that are part of the whole school approach to dealing with negative behaviour – your task will be to support decisions made elsewhere and this can be stressful if they run counter to your own beliefs and practices;

- the approaches adopted by the teacher(s) or others in the unit or department – you do not have the historical association that the teacher has with the punitive side of correcting bad behaviour, but you do possess more of a tradition of working with individual pupils and looking to advise and help them to generate their own solutions;

- the pupil involved – because you might feel that this was an unusual event for Jenny to be involved in, or Jackie is *always* in trouble and this is how we deal with her;

- your values and your own feelings about what has happened in the specific incident that you are dealing with;

- your own authority as a classroom or group manager – this can be based on the time worked in the classroom and a reputation that is hard earned or your natural skills in behaviour and controlling the classroom climate. Not all TAs want to be in control but would prefer to have an influence on the learning environment. The lack of the natural authority of the teacher role mentioned previously means that it is easy to feel threatened by defiance.

Punishment

In the early chapters the focus was on the power and authority of the adult as expressed through the system moving through to the more individual ideas which are less power assertive but require strong relationship-building skills. Punishment is associated with the more authoritarian end of the spectrum. There is a comfortable familiarity about the term 'punishment' and it is something that many adults experienced in schools. Whether the slap of a ruler, writing lines or detention, if not experienced personally, it has been observed by many TAs in their own schooling. After all it is a familiar word and tends to be expected by parents, the media and politicians. It offers clear messages that breaking rules will not be tolerated and it meets the needs of those wishing to see control reasserted. It also functions as a counter for the emotions aroused when a pupil's, or for that matter a member of staff's, rights have been violated. Think about your own emotions when someone who is close to you has been extensively bullied and your need to deal with the culprit and take control. In the everyday behaviour management in school TAs not only come across relationship issues such as bullying but also less aggressive threats such as those to the school rules and disruption which runs counter to the lesson objectives. These usually less emotive incidents need consistent handling and positive action but whether 'punishment' best describes that action is debatable. Even with the more emotive behaviours that are considered challenging punishment may not be a solution, especially with younger children (Bray and Lee, 2007).

Punishment indicates that the pupil is treated in a deliberately unpleasant manner and generates a dilemma as there are those who are not always comfortable about treating pupils in a way that might hurt them, albeit more socially and emotionally rather than physically as in bygone days. In contrast there is a view that it is exactly what is required. Pupils need to experience something aversive – or what is the point? Wilson (2002) argues that for punishment to be effective pupils should:

- acknowledge that what they have done is wrong;

- understand why it was wrong;

- understand the impact that they have had on others;

- feel a sense of guilt or shame for what they have done.

He adds that punishment should be unpleasant enough to counter the temptation to repeat the act. The four points above suggest questions/ statements that might be used prior to any form of punishment or sanction.

- *You have broken the rule on ...* (statement)

- *You do know that you have broken the rule on ...?* (question/statement)

- *Do you know that what you have done breaks the rule on ... ?* (question – likely only to be used where you have doubt that the pupil does not know the rule or is unsure of it)

- *Breaking that rule is wrong* (statement). *You do know that breaking the rule on ... is wrong?* (question/statement)

- *What you have done has hurt* (or *upset* or other more accurate description of the impact) ... (statement)

- *You do know that what you have done has hurt ...?* (question)

- *What do you feel about this situation?* (question)

What happens in the early stages has two purposes. First, it establishes what has happened and, therefore, the more 'statements' that are used the better. It allows for any anger or emotion, if there is any, to begin to subside somewhat if the approach adopted is a fact-gathering and listening one. Second, it functions as a rule reminder and reasserts the system put in place to celebrate success and deal with those who break the rules.

Despite the structure offered in the above TAs need to feel comfortable in carrying through the questions or statements and, more significantly, know that they can carry out the punishment stage in their own right and with the backing of others – in effect the system. Certainly in the early stages of the role this will be a challenging process and there is a need for developing skills in this task and securing the backing of others who may be more representative of the powerful forces within the system.

Notwithstanding arguments in favour and the skills that can be employed, there are downsides to punishment which require some reflection. There is always the danger that in the heat of the moment the pupil is labelled 'disruptive', 'bully' or even 'bad' when good practice demands that it is the behaviour that should be labelled. It can generate resentment towards the TA and to those who were involved in the original incident and, even worse, it can lead to anger and a desire for revenge. Punishment does not require a change in behaviour or any kind of restoration for those who have suffered and it can generate emotional distance from those who often need emotional closeness and trusted adult relationships the most.

In the context of the commentary above it is important to consider your own views on punishment through Exercise 4.4 and how this helps to meet the challenging behaviour of some pupils.

Exercise 4.4   What are your views on punishment?

This is an opportunity to reflect on this important issue and select statements that support your beliefs. Choose your favoured statement and give reasons for your choice in the middle column. In the third column add whether your views are those which are represented by the school in which you work. If none of the statements describe your views then create a fourth row in the empty one provided.

Statement	Reason for choice	Representative of school
Punishment is the best term to use and the way we should consider how to deal with non-compliance with the system. This is what happens in the real world.		
Punishment has strengths and weaknesses – at this stage in our development of the school I would like to look at alternatives and see if they have more to offer.		
Punishment is not relevant to the ambitions of this school and professionally I feel that there must be better ways of dealing with misbehaviour.		
Your choice		

Sanctions

'Sanctions' is the term used for a punitive action linked with specific misbehaviour or is the outcome of non-observance of a rule. It is a term often used in schools although there is a danger that it is little more than the old punishment in a new guise. Sanctions form part of the school policy which focuses on behaviour for learning and they should be designed to ensure that they are predictable and consistent. Authority comes from this part of school policy and the systems that support it and, therefore, TAs, as part of the school system, are able to draw upon its authority. Pupils know in advance the outcome of their misbehaviour and there is a logic to what happens to them. Effective sanctions are judged by whether they:

- match the misdemeanour;

- are designed to bring about changes in behaviour;

- prove to be a deterrent to the pupil or pupils concerned and the other pupils in the school.

There are always problems in imposing sanctions on pupils, especially when *you* are concerned about what you are doing, whether it is just and rightly targeted. Often in the act of reprimanding a pupil those problems become evident but there may also be solutions.

- **Problem**: Reprimand gives a message that it is the breaking of rules which is the misbehaviour, when emphasis should be *focused on the behaviour itself* and its impact on others.

- **Solution**: Always point out what has happened as a result of the behaviour and that it is also the breaking of a rule – in that order.

- **Problem**: The sanctions may focus on the surface behaviours and if rigidly linked to an offence leave little leeway for flexibility. For example, if a pupil is caught running in the corridor it could be for a very good reason so invoking the 'running in the corridor rule' sanction may not be appropriate.

- **Solution**: Look at the underlying reason for the surface behaviour: the important question is not 'what rule have you broken?' or 'what happens if that rule is broken? but 'why are you doing this? – there could be a very good reason for the behaviour.

- **Problem**: If they are applied wrongly, they just become punishment under another name. They can cultivate resentment and end up damaging relationships with support staff.

- **Solution**: Rogers (1990) focuses not only on rules but on their fairness. Ensure the process of rule construction involves many parties and the outcomes are consistently applied.

- **Problem**: Lee (2007) pointed out that overly harsh application of sanctions contradict the way learning is approached. When pupils make errors in their work TAs show them where they might have gone wrong and explain it again, maybe using different methods. Their intention is to seek to help pupils to understand what was wrong and how to respond effectively. This is not always the case when people are dealing with disruptive behaviour.

- *Solution*: If applicable, take time to ask questions such as 'what have you done wrong?', 'what is the rule on this?', 'what could you have done differently?'

In some instances it is not always the case that the form of admonishment is negative which appears to defeat the objective. Sometimes children want attention (see Chapter 5) and if they cannot gain that attention through positive behaviour they will misbehave to make sure their needs are met. Similarly, on a freezing cold day when compelled to go into the playground, some pupils will look to break that important 'dangerous play rule' which carries with it the penalty of standing in the room designated for such infringements which just happens to have a hot radiator in it!

One behaviour management feature that is becoming increasingly popular in schools is the use of the 'scale' (DfES, 2004). Often school systems have a scale that links numbers of misbehaviours and to a higher level of sanction. Scales such as first offence 'yellow card' but second offence 'red' means that the 'yellow' one may function as little more than a warning and not be taken too seriously. If that first offence is serious, then it may merit a serious sanction. Dixie (2007) suggests a five-stage 'gradation' could be used, with contacting the parents being the final sanction. This idea seems to have a lot of practical merit although, with more serious offences, there would obviously need to be earlier contact with parents. In addition, five stages allow behaviours to become established as 'normal' and therefore harder to change. However, in general, the principle of scales has much to commend it in that the pupil is invited to change their behaviour and given responsibility to do so, which is perhaps the most significant aspiration of effective behaviour management.

Sanctions need to be targeted justly and therefore are usually not applied to those who were not involved. However, pupils nearby may have taken no action but their inertia makes the TA feel that they were complicit and that sanctions should apply. This can be illustrated by an incident of playground bullying where there are clear perpetrators and victims but there was also a network of bystanders who knew what was happening and could have prevented the act. Research suggests that 85 per cent of playground bullying usually occurs away from adults but in the presence of bystanders (www. ccakids.ca/tvandme/english/parents/pdf/bullytools.pdf). Should the bystanders be part of the sanctions policy?

The manner in which sanctions are applied ideally should be calm in order to avoid causing more disruption through deploying the sanction than the original offence and, therefore, the time, place and audience will be significant. Sometimes it can prove necessary to wait a short while, even though your concern has been stated, although to wait for too long with young children can mean that the reason for the sanction may be forgotten. Given that many TAs have close relationships with specific pupils who may have caused trouble it is essential that sanctions are applied without resentment, a rule reminder is stated and the 'slate is wiped clean' after their completion. Finally, TAs need to make sure that in applying a sanction they are not punishing themselves and losing their own precious break time or giving up their own time. Extra time should be spent with those who deserve it.

Consequences

The focus on the system becomes slightly distorted when considering the third form of punishment, consequences, because more than other forms *they are linked to the disruption or antisocial behaviour* of the pupil and the pupil is required to recognise that link. Being linked to specific behaviours they possess a transparency for all pupils to see, even if they do not agree with them. Potentially consequences take a lot of the stress out of classroom and group management because they are not associated with your response to the pupil or their actions. How much less stressful does 'Lee, I see that by throwing the paper on the floor you have chosen to tidy the room later' appear to be when compared to 'Lee, what are you doing throwing litter on the floor? You make sure you pick it up right now and see me at the end of the lesson.' Of course, in the heat of everyday life in the classroom, it is not easy to think of an effective statement – indeed, even given the time to consider statements it is still not easy. Exercise 4.5 gives you the chance to respond to behaviours that are considered negative.

Exercise 4.5   Your consequence statements

Look at the list of misdemeanours, which are all from *genuine* behaviour policies, below. Compose a suitable consequence statement to match each one. (It is not as easy as it looks – not all misbehaviours have a natural or logical consequence!)

Misdemeanour	Your consequence statement
Passing notes	
Talking out of turn	
Chewing gum or eating in class	
Shouting out in class	
Wearing outdoor coats in class	
Throwing litter on recreational areas	
Causing damage to school equipment	
Constantly turning around	
Constantly leaving seat when not required to do so	
Making 'put down' comments to classmates	

Among the additional merits that consequences have is that they invite review and agreement among staff if they do not appear to be leading to improved behaviour and, like classroom or school rules, they can be displayed for reference. They can be structured hierarchically, although there are cautions about this mentioned in the previous section on sanctions.

The words that are most associated with them are 'natural' consequences or 'logical' consequences and although, like sanctions, they can be part of a formal behaviour management policy, they provide an opportunity for power and authority to come from the pupil's engagement with their own behaviour and the formal system. At the heart of the approach is a desire to teach pupils about the impact of their behaviour. One of the attractions for TAs is that whenever possible pupils are treated with respect and in a reasonable and calm manner. The onus falls on the pupil.

Kohn (2001) is among those who have concerns about consequences. First, it amounts to a member of support staff requiring a pupil to do something negative, therefore how far is it different to punishment? Second, there is a danger of mixed messages because, although consequences should be administered respectfully, the logical task that follows could still be harsh. Thus the message received by the pupil is a mixed one and could be considered punishment dressed up in a gentler guise. Finally, over-application of the 'logic' element leads to pupils undertaking highly punitive tasks. This may be illustrated in your results from Exercise 4.5 which may be strange, contrived, over-harsh (or the reverse).

With an agreed framework behind which TAs and teaching staff can unite, and that allows some individuality as long as it complements the approach adopted, the system takes the strain and frees the TA to concentrate on their pupil(s) and the learning. Whatever the choice adopted by the school for their system – and you as an individual within that system – there are three ways of approaching punitive action and, as well as distinctive features, there is a degree of overlap. It is all too easy to become bogged down in the technicalities and terminology. The key feature that determines the success of the system is the removal of the emotional heat of reprimand, which means that the TA's intervention does not cause more disruption than the original problem it was meant to overcome. Ultimately much will depend on who says it and how it is said and, therefore, there are no guarantees that ensure that the solutions will work. Perhaps the questions that need to be asked are: 'Do the methods I use change pupils' behaviour?' and 'Do I feel good about using these methods?'

Further reading

Drifte, C. (2008) *Encouraging Positive Behaviour in the Early Years: A Practical Guide*, 2nd edn. London: Paul Chapman Publishing.

Harrop, A. and Williams, T. (1992) 'Rewards and punishments in the primary school: pupils' perceptions and teachers' usage', *Educational Psychology*, 7 (4): 211–15.

McLean, A. (2003) *The Motivated School*. London: Paul Chapman Publishing.

Olsen, J. and Cooper, P. (2001) *Dealing with Disruptive Students in the Classroom*. London: Kogan Page.

Rogers, B. (2003) 'Behaviour consequences', in *Effective Supply Teaching*. London: Paul Chapman Publishing.

Rogers, B. (2004) 'The language of behaviour management', in R. Wearmouth, R. Richmond and T. Glynn (eds), *Addressing Pupils' Behaviour: Responses at District, School and Individual Levels.* London: David Fulton.

Rogers, B. (2007) *Behaviour Management: A Whole School Approach*, 2nd edn. London: Paul Chapman Publishing.

Visser, J. (2000) *Managing Behaviour in Classrooms.* London: David Fulton.

Wright, D. (2006) *Classroom Karma: Positive Teaching, Positive Behaviour, Positive Learning.* London: David Fulton.

Website

www.ccakids.ca/tvandme/english/parents/pdf/bullytools.pdf

References

Bray, L. and Lee, C. (2007) 'Moving away from a culture of blame to that of support based approaches to bullying in schools', *Pastoral Care in Education*, 25 (4): 4–11.

Department for Education and Science (2004) *Key Stage 3 National Strategy: Advice on Whole School Behaviour and Attendance Policy.* London: DfES.

Dixie, G. (2007) *Managing Your Classroom*, 2nd edn. London: Continuum.

Kohn, A. (2001) *Beyond Discipline: From Compliance to Community.* Upper Saddle River, NJ: Merrill Prentice-Hall.

Lee, C. (2007) *Resolving Behaviour Difficulties in Your School.* London: Paul Chapman.

Rogers, B. (1990) *You Know the Fair Rule: Strategies for Making the Hard Job of Discipline in School Easier.* Harlow: Longman.

Wheeler, S. (1996) 'Behaviour management: rewards or sanctions', *Journal of Teacher Development*, 5 (1): 51–5.

Wilson, J. (2002) 'Punishment and pastoral care', *Pastoral Care in Education*, 20 (1): 25–9.

Wright, D. (2005) *There's No Need to Shout: The Secondary Teacher's Guide to Successful Behaviour Management.* Cheltenham: Nelson Thornes.

5

The negotiation approach

This chapter focuses on the negotiation process between TAs and the pupils with whom you work. By the end of the chapter you will have considered and gained a better understanding of:

- what is meant by negotiation;
- responses to pupils;
- the four mistaken goals of behaviour and what to do about them.

Here the needs of the pupil are important but so too are those of the rest of the class and that includes teachers and the TAs themselves. After a discussion of what negotiation is, there is an evaluation of first responses and subsequent ways of reacting when pupils are being disruptive. This is followed by an analysis of the four goals of misbehaviour – attention, power, revenge and withdrawal – and what they mean in practical terms.

If the system is the 'macro' view then this chapter and the one that follows are more the 'micro' view, in that they are less concerned with decisions made on behalf of the whole school, department or group or with standards that are often defined by others. Herein the focus is more on individual and group needs. Negotiated approaches, sometimes referred to as 'contracted', are based on the idea that both the TA and the pupil have an influence on the situation and on how to secure the needs of the whole group, including the pupils, teacher and any other TAs, yet they must also meet the needs of the individual student who is causing disruption. We have seen from Chapter 3 that this would appear to be the preferred approach of many TAs, and also a high priority for teachers with less experience. If your answers to the beliefs inventory (Exercise 3.1) indicated that your beliefs are more those of a negotiator, you prefer practices which invite pupils to be given the opportunity to make choices and understand their decisions and the consequences of them. Your task is to help pupils to make wise choices, and to take more responsibility for their actions and not lose sight of their rights but also recognise that others have rights too.

What is negotiation?

The term 'negotiation' is often associated with work-based disputes and negotiators are those who bring about a solution to a problem linked to jobs or wages. 'Hard' negotiation can occur when the parties involved have no emotional attachment and there is no need for goodwill. The sometimes confrontational process of buying a house illustrates this as does any kind of large sales negotiation. These approaches are of no value for resolving disputes with people with whom you have a relationship, as there is a winner and a loser. Being a victor may lead to reprisals being central in the thoughts of the defeated and this form of negotiation is predicated on being manipulative rather than being honest. There is a significant difference in the classroom context where the ambition is not for one party to emerge victorious but for none of the parties to be defeated and for needs to be met on both sides, if possible.

The TA may be a negotiator between:

- the pupil and another pupil or group of pupils;

- the pupil and another adult (either TA or teacher);

- the pupil and the breaking of a rule.

It is often the case that negotiation is about seeking ways forward after incidents between TAs and the pupils. It then lacks the feeling of being a third party looking for a solution that is a 'win-win' for the other two parties, because you are on one side of the conflict that you are trying to resolve with all the attached emotions that are likely to be aroused.

Negotiation in schools is a process that aims to resolve situations where what the adult wants conflicts with what the pupil wants or vice versa. The aim is to find a solution that is acceptable to both parties, and that both sides feel that they walk away with something gained – hence the oft-stated 'win-win' situation, where both parties feel positive about what has happened once it is over. This helps people maintain good working relationships and fosters and develops teamwork once all has been resolved.

The climate and atmosphere of the classroom negotiation are central to its achieving its goals. High-level displays of emotions from the TA are unhelpful and inappropriate and, given that the pupil may be emotionally upset or even trying to manipulate the TA into being upset or angry, the message must be clear, calm, unrushed and assertive. On the subject of emotions, it is useful that the TA can discuss the feelings that they have and understand and acknowledge the feelings and emotions of the pupils. It is done in a detached way, but not a cold one.

Much is made in discussions of negotiation of the issue of position. The TA has a position which is what they require of the pupil in order that they and others can learn and enjoy their classroom. The pupil has another position, which can seem quite the opposite, but it is rarely as oppositional as it first seems. By exploring what they want or what their goals are you have the beginning of a 'give and take' situation. The language includes phrases such as 'we can do this when ...' and 'if we sort this out then we can ...'. Ultimately both the TA and the pupil feel comfortable with the solution and the 'win-win' has been confirmed. So much of day-to-day classroom behaviour management is based upon such ideas, especially for pupils seen as being difficult to control, and Exercise 5.1 invites extensive reflection on your experience of negotiation.

 ### Exercise 5.1   Negotiation questions sheet

1. Consider a classroom or school situation where you found yourself in what appeared to be a negotiating situation with a pupil. Write some brief notes on it.

2. Reflect on what happened using the questions raised in the second column. Write some more notes.

3. Could you have improved upon your actions or done things differently? If 'yes' say what could have been different.

4. Were there any major areas where you should celebrate your practice? Write down what they were.

Issue	Questions	Notes
Power	Who had the power in the situation? Who stood to lose the most?	
Relationship	What was your relationship with the pupil? Did this history have an impact on what happened?	
Goals	What did you need to get out of the negotiation? What did the pupil(s) need?	
Deals	What did you have that could be part of the deal? What did you want from them? What ended up being given away?	
Past	Does the pupil have a history of conflicts with adults? What was the history of outcomes in any past conflicts?	
Other routes	What alternatives did you have? How important was it to reach a negotiated position?	
Self-appraisal	How did you rate your performance? What were your successes? What might you have done differently?	

Keys to your success are having a plan for dealing with disruption, starting with considering your own reaction. Confidence in your own skills and an ability to work constructively through a series of steps means negotiation starts with the TA being able to predict their own behaviour and, consequently, predict more of the pupils' behaviour. Glasser's (1969) structured discipline plan was designed for teachers but has much to offer TAs, if requiring a little adaptation which includes reducing the number of steps. The statements below have more application to situations in which the TA is teaching or supervising away from the teacher or has a cover supervision role. The first three are about examining your skills and reactions before seeking a solution that will, hopefully, suit all.

1. Examine your own practice

If certain lessons or ways of working with pupils do not appear to be going well and they are misbehaving then examine your own techniques first. You may decide not to intervene but to wait and see if problems are going to resolve themselves and not become a distraction for the whole class. A natural reaction is to respond negatively immediately as soon as the disruption occurs while the opposite, i.e. doing nothing and seeing if the disruption disappears, is also a potential response. Doing nothing should be a deliberate first step.

2. Stop doing what does not work

So much of behaviour management boils down to not carrying on doing something when it is clearly not working. If, having examined your practice, you notice that your behaviour may be contributing to the problem then stop it. In some cases this is easier to say than it is to do, and nervousness can lead to some strange responses. You will no doubt have come across adults who seek to maintain a working noise level by constantly making a 'sshhhh' sound that ends up sounding like a steam train. Many adults have mannerisms which betray a lack of confidence – fidgeting with a collar, playing with your hair, looking anxious and unhappy – and for those who are new to the role of TA this is natural. But with experience and growing confidence these should be replaced with clarity of tone, confidence expressed through body language and a delight in your role that is conveyed to the pupils – most of the time!!

3. The positive behaviours

Notice the positive behaviours more than the negative. This idea finds itself in almost all books on behaviour yet still needs to be stated as research suggests that the balance between positive and negative in the classroom still needs to be redressed in favour of the positive. Some pupils make it hard for you to 'catch them being good', some have experienced little positive input in their lives and even appear not to enjoy celebration when they do things well.

4. Initial intervention

If the pupil disrupts your work with them, then respond sharply but not aggressively by asking 'what are you doing?' or 'what is going on?' The question invites clarification and response. In the case of older pupils 'don't do that' or 'stop that' may lead to you being ignored or even an aggressive reaction. In younger pupils it could prove successful to say such things as 'stop that' but it offers no explanation and means 'do as you are told' not 'this is what you are doing and this is why it is wrong'. Sometimes good behaviour approaches can feel more like *selling* good behaviour rather than *telling* about bad behaviour.

5. Second and third stages: inviting the positive responsive

Continued disruption should be met with the same type of response as the previous stage but this time with the added 'it is against the rules' or 'this is not what was agreed by the group'. If there is no positive response then stage three is something along the line of 'this is what I saw you doing and we know it is against the rules'. Up until this stage you have examined your practice and invited the pupil to react positively but now you are moving towards a more negotiating role and agreed rules are your support.

6. Fourth stage: 'working it out'

'We have to work it out' is the next step with the emphasis on finding a solution whereby the pupil follows reasonable rules and does not disrupt others. If no solution is found or agreed then the pupil should be withdrawn from the group and placed on their own within the classroom until a solution for being part of the group is worked out. If it continues they should be sent from the room to a designated place in the school. They must 'work it out' before being allowed to return. The essence is to give pupils time to agree a solution and move to a position where they have had their say and yet recognise that they need to work within an agreed framework that meets the needs of the group.

All of the above may appear too ambitious or too contrived when extreme anger is displayed or pupils become endangered by sudden outbursts. The principal function of this form of response is to help to distinguish between major and minor events, to be more reflective and to help deal with the day-to-day minor disruption that irritates so many adults and pupils.

Mistaken goals

Despite not always appearing so, a pupil's negative action invariably has some purpose to it and aims to fulfil a goal that they have set for themselves. One of the most helpful models for understanding pupil behaviour are what Dreikurs described as the Four Goals of Misbehaviour (Dreikurs, 1972). The underlying premise is that all pupil behaviour is goal led and has a purpose but when needs are not met those goals become more negative in form. From a pupil's perspective it is not always necessary for their behaviour to be positive or socially acceptable, and the dominant criterion which determines if a particular behaviour persists is whether it meets the child's need to belong. Hence, if children cannot find a place in their group through positive, cooperative behaviours they will often seek to achieve their aim by pursuing 'mistaken goals'. The four goals are:

1. attracting attention;

2. demonstrating power;

3. seeking revenge;

4. escape by withdrawal.

While there is a concensus in terminology in the literature for the first three, the fourth goal of 'withdrawal' is often described differently such as 'inadequacy', 'inferiority complex', 'avoidance of failure' or 'assumed disability'. This goal, whatever its title, serves as a reminder that pupils who present behaviour problems are not always those who are loud, aggressive or disruptive. It is all too easy to forget that behaviours that do not necessarily disrupt others or ourselves are nonetheless negative and they need our attention too.

When a TA states that they cannot understand why a child is behaving in a certain way, they are not aware of the purpose or goal of the pupil's behaviour. In seeking to find a particular goal you can analyse your own feelings and reactions to the pupil's behaviour and this will give significant clues, because your reactions often sustain, even strengthen, that negative behaviour. The key to improving a child's behaviour is to identify its purpose and then respond in such a way that the behaviour does not achieve its intended goal, or if it does it is on more balanced terms, in other words it is not at the expense of other pupils, the teacher or yourself. Acceptance of the idea that a pupil's behaviour has a purpose behind it means that it is possible to look beyond what is being presented by the pupil and seek the purpose by asking the question 'what is this behaviour trying to communicate to me?' From this, imaginative long-term solutions rather than short-term quick-fixes emerge.

The following review of the goals sees them as very distinctive, but support staff in schools reveal that often the first three – attention, power and revenge – are not easy to distinguish between, especially among some of their most diffcult pupils who may appear to exhibit more than one goal.

Attention seekers

 Case study: Tanya

Tanya always enjoys being at the centre of the class or group with her one objective being to be the star of the show. When she enters the room she immediately talks to her friends rather than sitting down and doing what is asked. She talks out of turn ('tooting'), is often to be found out of her chair and will argue when told to sit down. No matter what you say she will have the last word, although it is not personal as she does this to evey-one. Her contribution to group discussion is loud or again out of turn and she is prone to making noises just for the sake of it. Questions are answered but rarely correctly – indeed most of her comments appear quite random with lots of calling out and waving hands in the air. She finds it hard to share equipment and makes a 'big issue' of requests from her peers and staff.

In her work with you she constantly manages to engage you even when you are trying to work alongside others and much of what she has to say is irrelevant. Try to ignore her and she will disrupt everyone and provoke a reaction from her peers. However, it is not always negative as she can behave well – almost too well – and then you find yourself heaping praise upon her and constantly engaging with her. Whichever Tanya turns up, she always leaves you feeling exhausted and frustrated and the pupils in the group find it hard to concentrate.

TAs report that this is the most common of the four goals that they observe in their pupils. The pupil's sense of belonging is based upon the attention of others and they do not always feel that they get the attention that they deserve, therefore they gain that attention through annoying others and disrupting the group. Their behaviour can be aggressive – 'show-off', 'clown' – or defensive through being lazy, shy or desperate to help. They can be annoying or seem to need to be coaxed into action. One of the reasons that pupils misbehave is that they know how the adults will react and these reactions help to sustain and strengthen undesirable behaviour. In the case of younger pupils they may not know what the desired behaviour is, i.e. how you want them to behave. Just working with them to understand what is required of them is helpful. The aim of a TA is to help the pupil become supportive of others, contribute in positive ways to class teams and offer answers to questions but not be disappointed if their views are not selected.

Possible ways of dealing with attention seekers

- If the pupil is old enough, discuss the goal with them.

- In order to help them it is important to give them the maximum amount of positive attention to reinforce the behaviour you want. If you give extensive attention for positive behaviour and ensure minimal or no attention for negative behaviour, the pupil learns to get the attention they need in an appropriate way.

- Tactically ignore negative behaviour but notice the good behaviour of nearby pupils. Here is a good case for 'catching them being good'.

- In the case of younger children use more systemic approaches such as reward programmes, especially those which apply to all the class or group.

- Attention seekers can sometimes be looking for a role and it may be that giving them a specific role or level of responsibility can be useful.

- One slightly more 'left field' way of looking at the problem could be that you contract with the pupil to accept their negative behaviour. You allow the attention-seeking behaviour to carry on, even giving permission for it to do so. This is likely to work best where the behaviour is designed to irritate the adult as it becomes less attractive not to be annoying anymore.

- After explaining consequences make your expectations about their behaviour clear and reward compliance if appropriate: 'You are always talking during the lesson, you don't finish your work and you stop other children from getting on with theirs. This is not acceptable but I will support you when you concentrate on your work, try your hardest and allow others to get on with their work.'

Power

 Case study: Callum

Callum dominates the main social groups in the class. You know that whenever he is in your group he will be late and, when he eventually turns up, he will make a spectacular entry. When asked to sit down quickly and get on with his work, the body language will convey the response 'go on then, make me' – indeed it may be more than the body language! Much of his behaviour in class can be very defiant, even rebellious, often refusing to do what he is told. For example, when given the choice between work completion and staying in during the breaktime, Callum will refuse to do the work and then say 'you cannot make me stay in' with a few added expletives before his usual stormy exit. The more you confront the negative behaviour the more he appears to enjoy the challenge. On many occasions you have felt threatened by his attitude and behaviours and sought help from the teacher but the new young class teacher is often as anxious as you when Callum is around and she often turns to senior colleagues to deal with him. She feels that this is the only way she can ensure that her authority is somewhat secure. This passes the problem on but does not resolve it. Callum is aware of this and becomes aggressive, and he often has temper tantrums to avoid working with any support. In return, adults find themselves losing their temper and shouting 'I have had enough of this'. He really does push the boundaries and seems to have a personal agenda but when you ask other staff they say the same so it cannot be your fault!

Pupils who seek power need to feel in charge and will feel a failure if they do not win or their view of the world is not accepted as the right one. They enjoy telling others what to do but are not good at being given instructions themselves. They sometimes come across as bullies who are self-indulgent and who use anger and argument to control their world and can be disobedient and uncooperative. They are competitive and, when asked to stop, the pupil will continue to misbehave and begin a public power struggle with the adults who are supposed to be in charge. Their authority is challenged leaving them angry and yet vulnerable. Staff response is to retaliate against these not very likeable pupils, to want to engage them in a control battle or even to feel defeated by them. 'If you don't stop I will send you to the office' leaves no one feeling good about the experience – especially the office staff! Resorting to threats such as 'I'll teach you to defy me' leads to a power struggle and does not necessarily end with an adult victor. The aim of the TA here is to help the pupil to assume responsibility for their actions, to model self-discipline and to become a positive leader in the group.

Given that this book is about such issues as power and control in schools and classrooms, the power-seeking pupil illustrates many important questions:

- Can we let the pupil assert their power over their peers and, perhaps, adults?

- Is the answer to suppress the pupil with methods that they might employ themselves?

- Is it possible to balance matters – to give the pupil some say and some importance but only if it is constructive and non-threatening to others?

Possible ways of dealing with those who need power

- Listen first – let them have their say.

- Avoid getting caught up in the power struggle that the pupil sets up. There is no point in challenging a TA who does not rise to that challenge.

- Try encouragement as much as possible, particularly when linked to cooperation with others.

- Offer choices and negotiate time limits that are reasonable.

- Use circle-time to encourage cooperation, responsibilities and regard for the opinions of others. In a good circle all pupils have equal 'symmetric' power (Olweus, 1993) and it is safe to take risks and make mistakes.

- Once they are aware of the issue of their responsibilities offer consequences for misbehaviour as a choice: 'If you continue to upset Beth you will have to sit by yourself. The choice is yours.' 'I am disappointed Callum, but I did speak to you about letting Michael get on with his work. You have chosen to sit by yourself.' The pupil is then responsible for their behaviour and takes the stress of failure away from the TA, who has been assertive rather than aggressive.

- However hard it is, give them praise or encouragement, but not when behaving badly, just for being themselves. They do not have to perform to receive your celebration.

- Take an interest in them, their hobbies, hopes, interests and family. You may be one of the few people who does take such interest.

Revenge

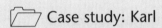 Case study: Karl

You have always trusted people, especially the young people that you work with, and, as a result of your approach you are quite open about your possessions. For example, although you do not leave your bag deliberately in the classroom, you do not get worried if you realise that you have left it in a vulnerable position. You trust people. However, recently several of your more personal possessions have disappeared from a drawer you use to store those sorts of items. What you find most surprising is that no money has been stolen. You are certain who is doing this – it is Karl. He is a student who you work with on an individual basis and you know his behaviour well although you would not say you were close to him.

He has a reputation for bullying young children. He is popular among a small group who hang around with him because the alternative may be to be his next victim. He constantly seeks to point out the differences in people and they can become the subject of his vicious humour, plus he is prone to blaming them for things that they have not done.

Despite this you believe in the principle that pupils like Karl are troubled and need more care and attention that others – you find him difficult, if not impossible, to like. Recently he was not well and was not at school and you feel the difference this made to your work and to the atmosphere in the class. It seems a terrible thing to say but everyone enjoys his absence.

The pupil's goal is to get even by hurting others in response to being mistreated by others in his own life. They hurt and they want others to hurt as well which means that they can find a place in the social group. These can be the brutal vicious tough guys and girls who arouse similar strong responses and oppositional stances. They can also be sullen, moody and refuse to join in. Their pleasure is the pain of others and they are very deliberate in their task of undermining others and damaging their feelings of self-worth. The ways that they gain their revenge may include stealing, physical assault, destroying property or being cruel and it often appears that they want 'two eyes for an eye'. The pupil who seeks revenge thrives on public admonishment as it confirms that they have the ability to arouse your feelings. The aim of the TA is to support the pupil in making positive relationships with pupils in the class who are not their closest of friends and to work cooperatively in your groups.

Possible ways of dealing with those who need revenge

- Give them some control by describing reality such as 'you're working well today', instead of 'I like the way you're working today'. It is sanctioning their control over their behaviour as well as offering some positive feedback. Here is good example of the pupil who needs more encouragement than praise.

- Avoid retaliation.

- Discuss the provocative side of their behaviour but in the context of a talking about the positive qualities they possess that can make others like them.

- 'Reframe' their actions and attribute positive reasons for their behaviour. 'I can see you have not finished yet, probably because you spent more time planning'.

- Remember not to react personally about their behaviour as part of their mistaken goal is to make you feel upset or hurt or as if they are ungrateful for your efforts.

- Where rules are developed ensure that they feel ownership of them and seek to create a sense of fairness for inappropriate behaviour.

- Avoid telling them off in front of an audience, however small that audience is.

- Keep calm and try to avoid responding emotionally to attempts to hurt or involve you in a battle of wills.

Withdrawal

 Case study: Rashid

There are few more frustrating pupils than Rashid and there are a number of concerns that you have about him. He is lazy and does not want to try at areas that he should succeed in, and his approach leaves you confused and concerned. He is often absent from school and you believe that many of his illnesses are minor or even non-existent.

Socially he is very isolated and is always by himself or on the outside of groups. He appears to have no friends and even acts as the class baby, which gets him noticed and blamed by the others which further fuels his bad feelings about himself. All the staff have begun to give up on him and even the head teacher was heard to say that she was 'at my wits end' with him. He looks unhappy, and resists the help of his friends and also of yourself and when you praise him he denies the value of what he has done.

In the classroom he starts each session with you by stating that the work is too difficult and he cannot do it. You have to sit right by his side if any written work is going to be done and he stops as soon as he feels you are not looking. You have tried every persuasion technique but he still does little, and seems to lack care for his work even for himself. He is a dreamer and appears to live in a world of his own, and somehow he manages to be absent even when he is in the classroom. One of your main concerns is that you feel that if he involved himself more, he could enjoy school and get a great deal from it.

These pupils feel inferior, are often solitary, will not mix, appear idle and want to avoid being involved. As a consequence the staff feel that they can do nothing for them or try to suffocate them with over-attention. Because they are not as demonstrative and threatening as pupils who employ the other goals they are not always seen as behaviour problems – but they definitely are. They can appear quite indolent but most of the time they just dismiss their failings as their own stupidity. They seem to have low self-esteem and very much an 'I can't do' mentality. In addition, they can be very immature and treated by the other pupils as the baby of the class who needs support at all times, while from the perspective of the support staff their immature or babyish behaviour leads to suspicion of late development. All in all they leave the TA with feelings of helplessness and frustration. The ambition of the TA with this kind of pupil is to help them to take risks, allow them to make mistakes and seek to enhance what appears to be fragile self-worth.

Possible ways of dealing with those who need to withdraw

- Look to enhance their self-esteem by noticing their positive contribution, even when they cannot see it themselves, and catch them being successful.

- If they want you to do everything for them, be careful. Do not 'rescue' or over-protect them, but instead encourage and value their attempts, not the end product. Whenever the opportunity arises indicate to the pupil that they are capable and will achieve with effort. They will be successful if they try hard.

- Make sure they undertake activities that have success built into them, and gradually feed in degrees of difficulty.

- Role-model that making mistakes becomes okay since everyone makes mistakes and we can learn from them. Work does not always have to be perfect or right and we learn through mistakes.

- Minimise the effect of making mistakes by taking the blame. 'I am sorry, I didn't explain that too well.'

- Encourage risk-taking in learning and avoid blaming them if the risk goes wrong – if they tried their best, then that is sufficient.

- Focus on success by analysing past success, and build confidence by noting their contributions.

Working with the goal

TAs reveal that the four goals are very useful in understanding their pupils, enabling them to focus on the behaviour and not the pupil and providing ideas on how they might react. As mentioned earlier, one topic that often emerges is the possible overlap between the goals in that staff feel that pupils behave in ways which suggest more than one goal and it is difficult to spot which goal appears to be the dominant one, despite the fact that there usually is one. Although somewhat simplistic, one technique that may be a useful indicator in recognising a specific goal is the adult reaction to the pupil behaviour.

If the TA feels:

- annoyed because of the lack of response from the pupil despite nagging, persuading, reminding and pointing out then the goal is likely to be attention-seeking;

- threatened then the chances are the goal is power;

- hurt or defeated then the goal is probably revenge;

- useless, frustrated and hopeless despite every effort then it is probably withdrawal.

 ### Exercise 5.2   Does work, could work or does not work

The practical ideas that follow each of the goals have been generated through a variety of sources and there will be some that you have tried or would be prepared to try. List them in the second column. Some you have tried and they have not worked or you feel that they do not match your beliefs and therefore you could not try them or you would find it difficult to try them. List them in the third column.

	Tried or will try	Failed or could not try
Attention		
Power		
Revenge		
Withdrawal		

Disclosing the goal

Dreikurs et al. (1998) advocate that one way to deal with mistaken goals is to confront the child with them, and what follows is a script that illustrates the kind of questions and comments that might help. Before considering them the nature of the meeting needs some planning. It should be a relaxed meeting away from other pupils and adults with you sitting at right angles to the pupil and adopting a neutral at worst and friendly at best approach.

> Tanya has been shouting out in class and looking to attract the attention of anyone who will give it. You have the chance to talk through her behaviour with her and it might go something like the illustration which follows. It moves from saying what you have noticed to suggesting reasons why she is behaving the way she is, which is a highly sensitive stage of the conversation. After seeking some form of consensus about what has been happening a plan is devised that aims to allow the pupil to have control over what will happen.
>
> **Stage 1: Inquiry** – 'Tanya, you have been shouting out, talking out of turn a lot today and disrupting others near you. Do you know why you do it?'
>
> **Stage 2: Explanation** – 'I think I know why you are behaving like that. It is because you want people to notice you and be your friend. You feel good when others see you and listen to you. Do you like being in the middle of the action?'
>
> **Stage 3: Agreement** – 'I realised that you were trying to gain our attention by calling out.' If denied, then follow up with 'I thought that was what you were doing but tell me *why* were you doing it?'
>
> **Stage 4: Disclaimer** – 'I cannot stop you behaving like this and disrupting us when we are working'. It is essential that the supportive feel of the conversation is maintained.
>
> **Stage 5: Partnership** – 'What I want is to help you to find a way of stopping the shouting out and allow everyone to work without disruption.' The plan then devised is based upon times when the pupil exhibits behaviours that seek attention, and discussions with them on how progress will be monitored.

Throughout this chapter the emphasis has been upon identifying why pupils behave the way that they do and negotiating ways in which they can change their behaviour so that they get on with their peers in a positive way, but not at the expense of the latter. Meeting the needs of all pupils as well as your own needs remains a core principle and is driven by a balanced view of classroom power. There are occasions when the needs of the pupil has to be the dominant concern and specific skills and ways of working come to the fore that are hard to use in group or class work but vital to effective individual support.

Further reading 📖

Bentham, S. (2006) *A Teaching Assistant's Guide to Managing Behaviour in the Classroom*. London: Routledge.

Dreikurs, R. (1972) *Discipline Without Tears*. New York: Dutton.

Fox, G. (2001) *Supporting Children with Behaviour Difficulties: A Guide for Assistants in Schools*. Oxford: David Fulton.

Hook, P. and Vass, A. (2002) *Teaching with Influence*. London: David Fulton.

Mellor, N. (2008) *Attention Seeking: A Practical Solution for the Classroom*, 2nd edn. Bristol: Lucky Duck.

Rogers, B. (2007) *Behaviour Management: A Whole School Approach*, 2nd edn. London: Paul Chapman Publishing.

References

Dreikurs, R. (1968) *Psychology in the Classroom*, 2nd edn. New York: Harper & Row.

Dreikurs, R. (1972) *Discipline Without Tears*. New York: Dutton.

Dreikurs, R., Grunwald, B. and Pepper, F. (1998) *Maintaining Sanity in the Classroom: Classroom Management Techniques*, 2nd edn. Philadelphia: Taylor & Francis.

Glasser, W. (1969) *Schools Without Failure*. London: Harper & Row.

Hook, P. and Vaas, A. (2000) *Creating Winning Classrooms*. London: David Fulton.

Olweus, D. (1993) *Bullying in School: What We Know and What We Can Do*. Oxford: Blackwell.

6

The relationship approach

This chapter focuses on the relationship between support staff and the pupils with whom they work. By the end of the chapter you will have considered and gained a better understanding of:

- why TAs are in an advantageous position to use the 'relationship approach';
- key skills in this area;
- a specific solution-focused approach;
- how to deal with anger;
- the importance of self-esteem.

Here the power of the pupil comes to the fore and their needs are paramount. After a consideration of the advantages that TAs possess in this area there is a sharper focus on listening and counselling skills before looking at solution-focused approaches which require these skills and more. The discussion moves on to dealing with a pupil who is angry and then provides an extended reflection on a significant area in terms of the relationship between the TA and the pupil – that of self-esteem.

This chapter considers a variety of ideas and approaches that help to bring the pupil's issues to the fore. It is based on the premise that pupils who misbehave may need support and help. Their irritating, rude or antisocial behaviour and their inability to understand its effect on others is often a manifestation of a deeper need. While the surface behaviour cannot be tolerated or condoned, especially if it has an effect on others, the underlying causes need to be understood and there is a need to bring about change in behaviour and circumstances. For the adult in a supporting role this requires skills

and approaches that put t̶ osive way. It
is not always easy as som̶ /ou to want to
support them, yet teachi̶ position to provide that much needed ̶ red by the pupil
aims to help them take more ̶ actions through
listening to their case in a non-judgem̶ ̶nd helping them
arrive at solutions that are possible and for which they feel a sense
of ownership.

The proximity of the TA: a major advantage

The role of support staff in schools has a history, albeit a brief one,
that was often associated with working alongside individual or small
groups of students, many of whom had special educational needs.
Much of their function was based upon their close relationship with
individual pupils and, because it proved so successful, it is still a common form of deployment of support staff. However, earlier in the
book there seemed to be an indication from the beliefs inventory
(Exercise 3.1) that they, like teachers, have fewer beliefs in the
'Relationship' element and were more linked to the 'Negotiator' and
'System' elements. This evidence suggests that, despite having a tradition of relationship-based approaches, the beliefs of TAs are based
on the other sets of approaches and raises potential tension between
practice and principles which may be shared by other professionals
in schools and needs some reflection.

Whatever the answers to these questions in many cases TAs have the
opportunity and time to talk matters through with their students.
They can find themselves in a position where they get to know certain pupils better than teachers do and with this proximity comes a
chance to prevent, defuse and understand behaviour problems. Such
opportunities also allow the TA to utilise skills that are akin to counselling to help provide a chance for the pupil's voice to be heard,
although the argument against this is that some pupils who exhibit
behaviour problems have no trouble in finding their voice! In many
cases the voice that is heard in the classroom is that of the troubled
individual who hides behind a mask that prevents the adult world
becoming aware of their underlying problems, as has been explored
in the previous chapter's discussion of mistaken goals. Additionally,
many pupils who exhibit poor behaviour and appear confident, even
over-confident, are often hiding poor feelings about themselves and
low self-esteem.

Throughout this chapter are ideas that focus on the individual pupil and their needs and responsibilities for their behaviour. What is essential is to recognise that, despite using ideas that have a thera-peutic or counselling basis, support staff are usually not qualified and are not employed as therapists or counsellors. Therefore their aims are not to create a therapeutic environment but to use the tech-niques and ideas to support behavioural change. There also needs to be an acknowledgement that teachers find it harder to fulfil their counselling and guidance roles as they are often required to focus on academic success at the expense of the wider aim to help develop fulfilled and productive citizens (Hornby, 2003). This contrasts with recognition that there is a growing need for pupils to receive guid-ance, individual support and some counselling. The skills of the TA provide the perfect opportunity to help provide balance in a world in which children can receive much advice and direction yet decreasing chances to be heard and supported in finding solutions and working through problems for themselves.

Listening

When analysing the skills involved in working with children and young people in a school environment, including those in dealing with disruptive behaviour, one thought is uppermost and that is that some people appear to have them in abundance. For others it seems that they have to be learned and this even applies to something as seemingly basic as listening, although most support staff are good natural listen-ers. However, it is not always *talent* that is linked to the skills, some-times it is the *context*. For example, a head teacher carries authority with the title and therefore perhaps commanding respect becomes an easier task. However, in the case of listening to children TAs are, as sug-gested above, in an advantageous position. Because they work more closely with the pupils, and often with individuals or small groups, they have increased opportunities to listen to the pupil and hear their stories and understand their agendas. It is important therefore to reflect on what listening entails in order to maximise understanding and skill levels because being sympathetic is only a small, albeit vital, compo-nent of effective listening. One key feature is to avoid seeing listening as a passive process but rather as a highly skilled operation, the key components of which are given below as a checklist.

1. *Ensure the environment is suitable*. Distractions are likely to be other pupils but could also be room temperature or poor ventilation.

2. *Avoid being distracted yourself.* Maintain concentration so do not respond to mannerisms, language, dress – indeed any side issues.

3. *Offer open support.* Help the pupil feel at ease with 'I'd like to help by hearing what you want say' or 'try to tell me about what's worrying you'.

4. *Check meaning and seek clarification when required.* You need to be clear about the concerns and an occasional 'did you mean that ...?' or a 'from what you say it seems that ...' type of statement which lets the pupil know that you are totally involved.

5. *Offer encouragement.* 'You are doing very well'. 'I appreciate the effort that you are making'.

6. *Ensure coverage.* Make sure that they are saying all that they want to say through 'is there any other important point that you may have missed out?'

7. *Reflect ideas and feelings.* By acting as a mirror for their feelings you help the pupil understand what feelings they are expressing to you: 'it seems that you feel ...' or 'you appear quite upset when ...'

8. *Summarise the meeting.* This brings together the central ideas that they have conveyed to you and provides a basis for action or future listening.

Two very important points need to be added here. First, included in the above list are suggested comments and questions that might be helpful. However, it is essential to add a note of caution that too many interruptions from you *can* lead to the feeling not of being listened to but quite the opposite – being interrogated. The good listener knows when to interrupt and how often – sometimes not very much at all. Second, it is essential to set the tone by establishing what might happen afterwards. For example, a pupil who is talking about why they cause disruption in order that another person may understand him or her may be doing so just to let an adult see their side of the story. It may end at that. However, a pupil talking about any form of abuse or bullying may tell you things that you know will require action. At the outset it is essential to establish, in clear, appropriate language, that you, like any other member of staff, are required to disclose information about any form of abuse. The issue of confidentiality sets the tone for what will follow and the discussion on counselling. The choices can amount to:

- total confidentiality – which amounts to no action, will be the result of the listening unless the pupil requests otherwise;

- partial confidentiality – in which it is established before the conversation or near the beginning that you intend it to be confidential but if you hear something that concerns you or senior staff need to hear you will have to take action but in a way agreed with the pupil. This is often the way that the reporting of bullying is dealt with;

- no confidentiality – whereby the pupil and yourself agree that you will pass on information or take action in ways that you will let them know and influence, i.e. who might be the best teacher, support worker or peer to talk to.

Counselling approaches

Many TAs, particularly those who work with individual or small numbers of pupils, find themselves in a close relationship with that pupil or with the opportunity for a close relationship to develop with that pupil. It is quite possible that this will be the best adult relationship that the student will have in their school years, and it can be a source of great comfort to them. Discussions with pupils after they have left school often reveal that significant adults such as support staff were the only ones that difficult pupils speak of with any affection. They were the adults who listened and gave them the chance to voice ideas privately without being judged. Many of the skills and approaches that are associated with the adult behaviour in these relationships resemble those which make counselling effective. In broad terms they include:

- the capacity to build a relationship in which the pupil feels valued, respected and accepted. There is a 'genuineness' and feeling of empathy which, while focused on the needs of the pupil, is often returned by a caring approach *from* the pupil towards the TA;

- the ability to help the pupil explore their own feelings, and personal histories with the aim of making sense of their situation and considering ways forward and opportunities for themselves;

- the opportunity to solve problems by *supporting* the formulation of objectives and plans for the future.

Such skills are based on being an effective listener, which is a role that support staff are frequently compelled to adopt through their more individual and affective focus. They can be broken down into verbal and non-verbal elements. In the case of the latter the following are essential:

- eye contact that shows engagement, avoids distraction but is not a stare;

- smiling and nodding the head at appropriate stages;

- hand gestures that emphasise and illustrate but are not distracting;

- reasonable speech rate and moderated tone of voice that avoids the loud or the hurried;

- close physical proximity but, in the contemporary litigious climate, avoiding touch.

The verbal elements include:

- showing supportive concern that indicates clear non-judgemental desire to help;

- making occasional interruptions that allow for clarification, restatements, summaries and reinforces – 'I understand', 'OK I get it', 'mmm, yes I see'. These reflect what the student is saying, provide necessary pauses and demonstrate attentiveness;

- using humour as a way of reducing tension but not in such a way that the humour dominates or detracts from the main purpose;

- trying not to react to anything that may be said that can shock or with which you disagree – it's essential to remain unaffected other than in positive ways;

- using first names;

- staying focused on the primary concern of the pupil and maintaining their focus on it as well.

Often the best ways to explore effective practice and how it relates to an individual's skill set is to reflect upon what is not helpful practice. On the non-verbal side there are such actions as looking or turning away, frowning, finger pointing, yawning, sneering and an aggressive or unpleasant tone of voice. In terms of the verbal behaviours, they are patronising, using overly intellectual language, blaming, preaching, straying from the primary topic, going on about self, over-use of questioning (especially 'why' questions) and offering too much advice (indeed the object is to get the pupils to advise themselves).

All the above skills can be practised and learned, although as previously stated, some adults seem to possess them naturally and in abundance. Many teachers possess them although their role in some schools doesn't always invite practising them, and it is easy to be critical if they do not always appear to demonstrate them. Those who have to meet many classes and subjects in a single day, indeed day after day, are often compelled to utilise the more systemic elements of behaviour management and TAs are often better placed to exhibit their relationship-based skills. Thus it may not only be the values that each professional possesses but the environments in which a variety of values can exist.

What follows is an exploration of the *solution-focused approach* that, while much more specific and structured than what has been described above, draws upon pupil-centred support and illustrates important stages that can inform the support worker. It offers a regime that is enhanced by listening and counselling skills but in a specific and structured way.

A solution-focused approach

In recent years the solution-focused approach has enjoyed a higher profile in the work of those dealing with difficult behaviour in schools. It is important at this stage to say that it is not advocated here that TAs adopt this and no other way of dealing with difficult behaviour in a classroom context, but that a solution-focused approach has much to offer the TA who has an opportunity to engage in the potential for changed behaviour with pupils who appear to be constantly causing trouble. It is a way of working that has been integrated into the Behaviour and Attendance Strategy (DCFS, 2005a) because it is a 'positive problem-solving model … in which energy is directed towards finding satisfactory ways forward rather than focusing on what is going wrong in a situation.'

The principles that underpin the solution-focused approach have relevance to any form of support for change in a pupil's behaviour and are worth consideration, even if not applied in the formal way.

1. Solution focused: emphasis on the future not the past. So much of what is described as behaviour management considers the past and the pupil's record of disruption. The solution-focused approach has less emphasis on what the pupil has done and more on what they might do in the future. This does not mean that the past is not discussed at all but the emphasis is more on past successes not failures.

2. Seeking exceptions. It is important to help the pupil find contexts – times, places and people – when there were no problems. It could be working with a different social group, adults, lessons, time of day. What is essential is highlighting that there have been times when the pupil's behaviour was good and they had some control over it.

3. Pupil's power within. Here the TA would support the pupil in determining their potential to change and the positive features that they have. De Shazer (1985) sees this as the key to this approach and in this context it would mean the pupil sees that they can change their behaviour. This may seem less relevant in the context of minor disruption but highly significant in the case of a child who is appearing to withdraw or is experiencing bullying.

4. Small change will do. The emphasis here is upon a small change in behaviour that can break the pattern and lead to other more substantial changes later. For the pupil it may be that it is not just about change in behaviour but seeing their behaviour as different.

5. Goal-centred. Goals that will bring about changes in behaviour, circumstances or environment need to be set by the pupil. They may not be achievable speedily and the role of the adult here is to help make the goals achievable through graduated steps, with the emphasis on strengths and ways of coping.

6. Cooperation. In this case cooperation refers to the way in which the adult works with the pupil at times when they wish and places the concerns of the pupil at the centre. Language is important here and the terminology of the pupil is not judged. Even in questioning careful thought is given to language with emphasis on the positive. For example, when working alongside a pupil whose behaviour means they have been excluded from the class, questions

will focus on 'when you are allowed back what ...?' rather than 'if you are allowed back ...'

In summary, the solution-focused approach is not:

- based upon past failures but on past successes;

- explaining problems but considering progress;

- eliciting weakness and failings but isolating strengths and resources;

- looking at blaming others but acknowledging those who have contributed to the solution.

The process is divided into eight stages (see Table 6.1) and, as with the principles above, they are useful individually to reflect on but warrant consideration as a whole approach. The key techniques in Table 6.1 illustrate the careful, positive and future orientation of the process and here are accompanied by indicative examples of questions.

The use of a numerical scale (see 'Scaling' in Table 6.1 and Figure 6.1) has many merits including helping those pupils who may find it difficult to evaluate their behaviour in words, providing an easy way of comparing periods of behaviour, recording performance and inviting questions.

One of the many positive features of the solution-focused approach is that it helps to counter the helplessness that many pupils feel who seem to attract trouble and constantly feel distressed. They are supported through the development of techniques that help them to overcome their own problems and their agendas are central. However, as with all specialised approaches, there are cautions. Not all pupils are suited to the approach and, for those TAs entertaining the idea of

Where would you place your behaviour on the following scale
(1 = is very poor indeed and 10 is very good)?
What would be a good number to aim for?
What will your behaviour be like when you get there?

1 2 3 4 5 6 7 8 9 10

Figure 6.1   Scaling.

Table 6.1 The solution-focused approach: stages and key questions

Techniques	Key questions
1. *Other people's perspectives.* How others would recognise change.	What will your teacher see you doing that will be different? What will your friends see you doing that will be different? Who else will notice?
2. *Exception finding.* When things were better or handled well.	When was the last time that things went well? When did you feel good about being at school? When was there less of a problem?
3. *Scaling.* Attempts are made to quantify the problem (see Figure 6.1).	On a scale of 1 to 10, with 1 being the worst things have been and 10 being how you want things to be, where are you now? What tells you have moved from 1 to _? What would be a reasonable position to aim for now?
4. *Locating resources.* An appraisal is made of skills and strengths and who was helpful.	Who else will notice it when you are doing well? What will they notice? What helped you to do that? Who helped you to do that?
5. *Coping.* How pupils are coping and what or who is supportive.	How do you deal with it? Who helps you? What skills did you use? When are things OK?
6. *Stop things getting worse.* The need for additional support to provide an initial coping device.	Who would you be happy to have to help? Who can help to provide support?
7. *Constructive feedback.* Throughout it is important to keep the pupil in touch with what they are doing well.	You have been good at … You have helped me by being … You have kept going very well. That was a great idea and it has worked well.
8. *Ending.* Reminds pupils of indicators of progress and refers to goals stated at start of session.	We agreed that we need to look out for … We started by saying that … We decided that things would be improving if…

using it fully, it is important to undertake training and critically evaluate its use. It does not detract from the influence that it might have on other relationship-based approaches.

Anger

When a child is angry and that anger is expressed openly, which is often the case in school situations, opportunities to negotiate are unlikely to exist and the power of the system to influence their behaviour is very limited. An angry pupil has little or no self-control, and this situation tests the skills of the adult to the maximum. Using the key idea pursued throughout the book of who has power in these circumstances it is certain that the adult has very little power or control and, in cases where there is a complete loss of temper in the pupil, their behaviour may be powerful but pupils do not have control. The difference between *control* and *power* is an important distinction here. Outbursts of anger are invariably caused by frustration, through wants or needs not being met, or as a release to get rid of pent-up emotions. Confronting genuine anger with adult anger or frustration will do little other than add fuel to the fire. Whatever the origins self-control by the adult is essential, not only because little is achieved by an angry outburst from all parties, but also because it provides a good role model. The outburst calls upon an understanding of the relationship between adult and pupil and the capacity of that adult to understand what is happening, deal with it effectively and not be drawn into what is already a complex emotional agenda. What is required is not only calm but also clarity of purpose – the TA knows what is happening and can predict when the anger will subside and the next phase can begin.

At the heart of dealing with temper loss and extreme anger is:

- the TA's knowledge of the pupil;

- their own patience and attitude;

- their capacity to deal with the situation in the context of other pupils nearby.

Whatever is happening, it is important not to react negatively or to re-engage immediately with the issue that prompted the outburst when things have calmed. Loss of temper and extreme anger can be a highly volatile situation but it is also likely to have certain phases and reconciliation. Knowledge of what the likely pattern is will help to bring about the first steps to resolution.

Breakwell (1997) proposes that there are phases to anger. It is a helpful model as it provides some predictability in an unpredictable situation.

1. *Trigger.* This first phase is probably the best opportunity that the TA has to influence events. Temper loss is not just a threat to possessions or body but to precious self-esteem, which once damaged is not easy to repair, hence the importance of intervention, if possible. Before the pupil becomes incapable of listening to reason, some techniques that merit trying are distraction, relocating the pupil, relocating yourself – if you are threatened or part of the problem, move closer, use humour, make positive statements and maintain positive body language.

2. *Escalation.* The initial warning signs of raised voice or frustrated or aggressive body language in the pupil are replaced by more extreme physical and emotional reactions. Using Breakwell's metaphor of the firework to describe incidents of anger, the fuse has been lit. The greater the TA's knowledge of the pupil the more indication there is of whether they possess a short or long fuse.

3. *Crisis/outburst.* At this stage the pupil is incapable of seeing another person's point of view or of making rational judgements. Here the skill is maintaining the situation to ensure that there is no damage to the pupil, their peers or property. This is not an easy task and can sometimes be frightening but at this point calm, clear and consistent adults are the best way of generating those characteristics in the pupils. Other suggestions include the following:

   - Keep talking.

   - Check exits.

   - If things get too serious use those exits and seek aid from those in greater authority.

   - The removal of an audience is essential as is the removal of anything that could be a potential weapon.

   - If engaging in conversation or simply monitoring their behaviour, try standing next to the pupil, looking in the same direction as them, avoiding eye contact for the moment.

–   If there is a need for physical intervention, then it is important that it is in compliance with the school's restraint policy.

4. *Recovery or plateau.* Despite signs that the anger has begun to subside the pupil may still be vulnerable and confused. Crucial to the management of this phase is the timing of adult intervention, as it can take up to an hour before the rebuilding can begin – certainly it will probably take more time than you realise (Faupel et al., 1998). In terms of the firework analogy, never return to a firework that appears to be still alight.

5. *Post crisis or depression.* The skills required at this stage match those of other phases and yet the pupil is often left to their own devices, maybe in isolation. The realisation of what has happened and what might result from their anger leaves the pupil anxious and, significantly, they may display fractured self-esteem or feel depressed.

Knowledge of the stages is helpful in making predictions at an uncertain time but, when emotions are running high, there is the caution that every pupil, context and reaction can be different. A further factor that can impact on dealing with anger – indeed with dealing with other forms of disruptive behaviour – is how the adult feels about dealing with conflict and aggressive behaviour. Teachers may perceive an angry outburst as a challenge to their authority, but having less authority in the system may be a benefit for someone in a support role. The TA who brings calm, trust and understanding of the pupils and the nature of anger itself will approach the situation with confidence and strong self-awareness.

Self-esteem

It is a rare day in a school when an adult is not heard to say something about a pupil's self-esteem or self-image and the impact it has, either positive or negative, on learning, behaviour or both. These are terms that are often used without knowing their complexity and their potential to help pupils. Increased understanding of all the various elements of the subject provides a sound basis for working with and supporting pupils whose needs, such as those covered in the previous chapter, can lead to disruption in the classroom. The Social and Emotional Aspects of Learning (SEAL)

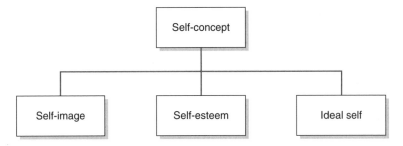

Figure 6.2 Lawrence's model of self-concept.

(DfES, 2005–6) initiative in England and Wales has developed the theme of 'Understanding Myself' with a focus on building individual relationship strengths, giving and accepting feedback from others and helping them. Among its aims is to support young people with a low sense of self-worth and to help them respond more positively to criticism. The link between SEAL and the Behaviour and Attendance Strategy underlines the importance of relationships and the link between positive self-esteem, good relationships and behaviour.

There are two areas of self-esteem that it is important to have some insights into and which help in understanding practice. First, there is the definition of self-esteem and the related terminology and, second, whether we place too much or too little emphasis on its significance. These are among the ideas discussed below.

Many attempts have been made to define what is meant by terms such as 'self-concept' and 'self-esteem' and a number of models have been developed. Lawrence's (2006) useful model distinguishes between its various components with self-concept being the overarching 'umbrella' term that embraces the three elements of self-image, ideal self and self-esteem (see Figure 6.2). TAs are in a position to influence these and, in some cases, they will be the primary influence.

Self-image is defined as the perceptions people have about themselves, not just in terms of appearance but also their abilities, personality and characteristics. It is determined by many factors and included are the relationships with significant others, especially in the early years. Other relationships might include support staff in educational settings. In the case of older children, it is likely that close relationships with specific TAs will have significant influence.

Cooley (1902) used the phrase 'looking glass self' where other people provide a social mirror and children come to see themselves as they are reflected in it.

- I am not what I think I am.

- I am not what you think I am.

- I am what I think you think I am. (Coopersmith, 1967)

Ideal self is what the person would like to be and their hopes and aspirations in terms of appearance, abilities, personality and characteristics. It combines collected life experiences plus the feedback from others.

Self-esteem is the discrepancy between self-image and ideal self. A pupil with high self-esteem will have a positive self-image and realistic hopes and aspirations which they feel they can achieve. Conversely, a pupil with low self-esteem has a negative self-image and unrealistic ambitions which they know they are unlikely to achieve given how badly they feel about themselves. They feel that they are not valued, cannot learn and have very little to offer. As a result they often act out and misbehave, sometimes hiding behind a 'mask' which hides their low sense of self-worth. TAs are usually able to see this and know the real person behind the mask, and the strength of the relationship supports the pupil at a time when the standard of their behaviour appears to be declining. You may recognise some pupils (even some adults!) in undertaking Exercise 6.1.

 Exercise 6.1   Masks your pupils put on

Consider the list of masks below.

1. See if you recognise a pupil or maybe some pupils who appear to wear them.

2. Consider that pupil's self-esteem and what you think it is.

3. Think about ways in which you can begin to remove the mask and relate to the real person behind it.

4. What are the skills that are required by the TA to achieve this?

Mask	Behaviour	Say such things as …
Helplessness	These pupils get everyone else around them to do their work, to help them and to rescue them. They refuse to take risks because they might fail.	'I don't understand', 'I can't do anything', 'I'm such a failure'
Super-competence	They can talk their way through any situation and may have some skills, especially those linked to manipulating people, and they can convince others and themselves that there are no real problems.	'everyone knows that', 'it's easy'
Invisibility	They look frightened, whisper to teacher and aim to ensure that they are never picked out.	'please don't see me'
Clown	Everything's a laugh when this pupil is around and they are the entertainers.	'what a joke', 'everything's a riot'
Victim	These pupils adopt the 'poor me' attitude and assume no responsibility for anything.	'it's not fair', 'everyone picks on me'
Not bothered	They do not risk failure. If they try to succeed and fail, they say that it did not matter anyway. With this mask they are never vulnerable.	'I don't care', 'it doesn't matter', 'who cares?'
Boredom	Their boredom usually masks frustration that they cannot do what they have been asked to do.	'this is boring', 'how long to go before break?'

(Continued)

(Continued)

Perpetual motion	Their constant activity wards away others and keeps them from having to perform.	'I'll do whatever you want later', 'later later ... no time now'
Outrageousness	Wild image and extreme approaches mask what they are really worried about – they know it is only a front.	'I'm way out'
Good Samaritan	They will be helpful to get out of doing what they know they will have problems with.	'let me help you', 'let me run the errands'
Contempt and blame	They are angry at the whole world for making them feel stupid.	'they don't how to teach', 'this pencil is useless', 'this school is useless'
Sporty	Their prowess in sports hides their failings in learning.	'I only love football, it's all that matters'
Perfection	They show no tolerance of their own problems.	'great artists don't have to read anyhow'

The role of the TA

Parker (2009) has pointed out that some TAs with whom she has worked convey a discrepancy between their own self-image ('uneasy', 'lacking in confidence') and ideal self ('self assured', 'confident' and 'outward going') and, therefore, it is logical to deduce from what has been stated before that they may lack self-esteem. This raises an interesting question – does the TA lack self-esteem because of their own feelings of poor self-image or is it that TAs possess low status and power in their schools and so it is the professional group that lacks self-esteem?

It is here that it is appropriate, through Exercise 6.2, to be a little more introspective and take the opportunity to reflect upon yourself – or maybe it should be written 'your self'.

Exercise 6.2   Powerful quotations

Many people have written about the concept of self, especially in relation to achievement, and below are several quotations made by famous people from all walks of life taken from one of the many websites on self-esteem (www.spiritwire.com/selfesteemquotes.html).

1. Read through the list carefully.

2. Select five that resonate for you and rank them in order in the column headed 'Me' – put 1 next to your favourite, 2 next to the second favourite and so on to 5.

3. In the notes column write why these five quotations resonate for you.

Quotation	Author	Me	Notes
It ain't what they call you, it's what you answer to.	W. C. Fields		
There's only one corner of the universe you can be certain of improving, and that's your own self.	Aldous Huxley		
You yourself, as much as anybody in the entire universe, deserve your love and affection.	Buddha		
The hardest challenge is to be yourself in a world where everyone is trying to make you be somebody else.	E. E. Cummings		
The way you treat yourself sets the standard for others.	Sonya Friedman		
Self-love is not so vile a sin as self-neglecting.	William Shakespeare		
Self-confidence is the first requisite to great undertakings.	Samuel Johnson		
You really have to look inside and find your inner strength, and say, 'I'm proud of what I am and who I am, and I'm just going to be myself.'	Mariah Carey		
High self-esteem isn't a luxury. It's a necessity for anyone who has important goals to achieve.	Jack Canfield		

(Continued)

(Continued)

You have to expect things of yourself before you can do them.	Michael Jordan		
Never bend your head. Hold it high. Look the world straight in the eye.	Helen Keller		
Whether you think you can or whether you think you can't – you're right.	Henry Ford		
Put all excuses aside and remember this: *you* are capable.	Zig Ziglar		
There is nothing noble about being superior to some other man. The true nobility is in being superior to your previous self.	Hindu proverb		

Self-esteem: the only answer?

Mention was made earlier about the potential overemphasis on self-esteem, and it is important here to make a clear statement about the subject. It is not suggested here that raising self-esteem provides a universal panacea for all behavioural issues in schools and that all pupils who misbehave have low self-esteem or vice versa. Similarly it is not suggested here that all pupils with high self-esteem are models of good behaviour. Critics of the overemphasis on self point to connections between high self-esteem and antisocial behaviour (Furedi, 2004) and it is all too easy to attribute disruption to ideas of self. 'High self-esteem is ... very unlikely to be the all-purpose social vaccine that some have supposed it to be' (Elmer, 2001: 59). This book is a challenge to anyone who is looking for a single solution to behaviour difficulties and is an advocacy of multiple approaches and multiple solutions from staff with a wide range of skills. Where there is agreement between the pro and anti self-esteem lobby is that, once formulated, notions of self are hard to change. It is also likely that parents are the main determiners of the formulation of a young child's self-image but later in their lives there are other significant adults who may be able to make a difference. Where there can be no doubt is that the list of approaches identified in Exercise 6.3 below can contribute to a stronger relationship with pupils that enhances their positive feelings about themselves and helps them to formulate realistic targets. Enhancing self-esteem may not be the only or best solution but pupils who do not value being valued and do not value being recognised are few in number – the same could be said of TAs!

Suggested actions

In keeping with the key themes advocated in this book it is essential that any action designed to improve feelings of self-worth should blend with *your* values, *your* skills and *your* ideas, and it follows that you make these clear – if only to yourself! It is also important to reflect upon what you are already doing. If self-image is altered by the interactions that pupils have in their everyday lives in schools then how significant adults such as TAs act and respond could be a major contribution.

 Exercise 6.3 Working on self-esteem

Look at the list below of suggested actions that could have a positive impact on pupils' self-esteem.

1. Using a 0–10 scale where 0 = 'I never do this' and 10 = 'I always do this' put a number against each action.

2. In the two empty rows at the bottom of the table add your own suggested actions that you have tried or you think would work if you tried them.

3. Look at each suggested action and see if you think they are more likely to help self-image (SI), ideal self (IS) or both (B). Write SI, IS or B next to each action.

Suggested action		Scale
1.	Make more positive than negative comments to your pupils.	
2.	Listen to them carefully.	
3.	Encourage the development of an accurate yet positive self-image.	

(Continued)

(Continued)

4.	Ask them to say what they want to achieve ensuring it is realistic.	'
5.	Do not be judgemental.	
6.	Invite them to take risks in classroom tasks.	
7.	Negotiate and agree realistic targets.	
8.	Place emphasis on effort before achievement.	
9.	Give high levels of encouragement and positive feedback.	
10.	Be a good role model and avoid running yourself down in their company.	
11.	Catch them being good and celebrate success.	
12.	Encourage positive feedback among peers.	
13.	Seek to foster unconditional positive regard.	
14.	Compare their work with previous work – not other pupils'.	
15.	Compare their behaviour with previous behaviour – not other pupils'.	
16.	Have positive expectations about their work and behaviour.	
17.	Create as many opportunities to succeed as is possible.	
18.	Develop and encourage resilience.	
19.	Foster an 'I can do this' approach in their tasks.	
20.	Give regular affirmation – daily if possible.	
21.	Support acceptance of mistakes.	
22.		
23.		

Among the actions given in Exercise 6.3 there is the advice often mentioned in the literature on behaviour management and stated before in this book, that is 'catch them being good'. Many pupils will be introduced to TAs who will work with them and these pupils will carry a history of negative labelling. They will be the 'naughty', 'impossible', 'helpless' and 'hopeless' and they will have embraced these labels, seeing themselves in a negative way and behaving accordingly. This provides opportunities for TAs to break the negative mould by:

- noticing their successes, positive contributions and caring behaviours;

- making sure they hear you make positive statements to your colleagues or other students;

- reminding them about their past successes.

This is even more effective if undertaken by agreement and as a group. On a personal note, when I was working in a special school the staff were shocked one day to see the file of a teenage girl, Debbie, who was about to join the school. The document was thick and full of descriptions of behaviours and events that suggested the label 'troublemaker', and quite a violent one at that. After extensive discussion and examination of the file the staff faced two choices – accepting the inevitable and dealing with what will happen or ignoring the tone and most of the detail on the file and treating Debbie in every way positively. The latter choice proved a resounding success and Debbie joined the school, adjusted quickly to her environment and presented as a 'model pupil', exhibiting none of the behaviours that had been anticipated. It was a testimony to the idea that enhanced self-image and boosted self-esteem can bring a change to behaviour. It was also a reminder that a troublemaker in one context can be something very different in another – just ask those who work with individual pupils in multiple classrooms as in most secondary schools.

A further suggested action is less easy to carry out but just as important and that is the emphasis on risk-taking. It is a means by which pupils can find out about themselves and the TA can find out about them. Linked to this is the idea that it is permitted to make mistakes and that mistakes are the key to learning. Through their own efforts pupils learn (1) that making a mistake is a learning process and (2) that effort matters, and that pupils who attribute their success or failure to that effort are assuming greater responsibility for their learning and behaviour. Often associated with enhancing self-esteem is the use of circle time, which permits the taking of risks and the offering of opinions without fear of arousing criticism or negativity. Any member of staff who uses any form of quality circles needs to be skilled in the techniques that make risk-taking safe from criticism from those in the circle. As with any technique used in schools, poor skill level and lack of understanding of the primary purpose of the technique can do more damage than good and circle time provides a prime example of this warning. Mosley and Tew (1999) point out that among the techniques that make circle time work is ensuring that everyone is safe from:

- overt criticism;

- mockery;

- being 'shown up' by staff;

- 'put downs';

- being named in a negative way.

Ensuring safety from the above comes from the experienced management of circles, and those who achieve this possess the potential to create an environment that is both safe and liberating for pupils. What is worthy of note is that the five bullet points above should not only be among the criteria for successful 'circles', but also seem essential to successful classrooms and schools.

Being pleasant to pupils would appear to be sufficient to ensure a positive relationship which provides a basis from which to deal with disruptive behaviour. Unfortunately, it is not that simple. Lawrence (2006) looks at the personal qualities that are desirable for teachers and there is no reason why these qualities should not be relevant for TAs. They have their foundation in counselling approaches and were mentioned earlier in the chapter:

- **'Genuineness'** is the capacity to be 'real' and not seek refuge behind a professional 'mask' – this would appear to be much easier for TAs than their teacher colleagues. The lack of a historical professional identity for support staff gives them advantages over teachers, some of whom act as teachers rather than being themselves in a teaching role. Pupils perceive this, and your genuineness can function as the other side of the 'you are just a TA' coin.

- *Empathy* amounts to knowing how the other person feels and can be learned by aiming to understand the feelings behind what the pupil is saying. So much of successful classroom management is based upon looking beyond the immediate and obvious behaviours for the reasons and background. Pupils are more likely to behave, achieve and enjoy learning with you if they feel they are listened to and understood.

- *Acceptance* is being accepting of the pupil's personality and avoiding being judgemental. It is not what they *do* that is accepted but who they *are* and the link with self-esteem is clear. Consider the following scenarios:

Scenario 1

TA   You are naughty talking when the group is trying to work in silence.

Pupil Sorry Miss.

TA   You are always disrupting the group and you get on my nerves.

Pupil I don't like you and don't want to do any work.

Scenario 2

TA   I get upset when you are talking and the group is trying to work in silence.

Pupil Sorry Miss.

TA   This is not the first time and we need to do this work quietly and without distraction.

Pupil I am sorry and I will try not to talk again.

In the first scenario the message is directed at the pupil and features the accusatory 'you', but in the second scenario the message is personalised and the TA emphasises the situation, the impact of the behaviour and her feelings through the 'I' message in 'I get upset'. The aim of this is to preserve self-esteem and not threaten the precious relationship between support staff and pupil.

The discussion in Chapter 4 included the subject of punishment and there would seem to be few harsher punishments that a TA can carry out than to threaten the relationship between themselves and their pupils. It would be a last resort, and serve little purpose in helping the pupil.

Conclusion

There is no doubt that the relatively recent SEAL initiative (DCSF, 2005b) has sought to put the emotional component of the education agenda at the forefront. Efforts to increase the vocabulary of emotions and the opportunity to express them are to be celebrated. Perhaps one of the problems that led to the initiative was a perceived lack of emphasis on matters emotional in the curriculum. Such a view echoes what many TAs report, that schools are driven by the need to provide successful examination data and ensure a compliant culture and system that meet the inspection framework. The agendas are formulated and assessed outside school, which means the ideas on caring can also feel imposed. TAs, support staff and teachers are, in the main, caring individuals by nature and know the value of the relationship element of education but they find it hard to prioritise it and so often see it as separate from the academic side of their work when it is really central.

Further reading

Barrow, G., Bradshaw, E. and Newton, T. (2001) *Improving Behaviour and Raising Self-Esteem in the Classroom: A Practical Guide to Using Transactional Analysis*. London: David Fulton.

Faupel, A., Herrick, E. and Sharp, P. (1998) *Anger Management: A Practical Guide*. London: David Fulton.

Hall, C. and Hornby, G. (2003) 'Learning to collaborate: working across the divide', in C. Hall, E. Hall and G. Hornby (eds), *Counselling Pupils in Schools: Skills and Strategies for Teachers*. London: RoutledgeFalmer.

Humphreys, T. (1993) *Self-Esteem: The Key to Your Child's Education*. Dublin: Gill & Macmillan.

Long, R. and Fogell, J. (1999) *Supporting Pupils with Emotional Difficulties*. London: David Fulton.

MacGrath, M. (2000) *The Art of Peaceful Teaching in the Primary School: Improving Behaviour and Preserving Motivation*. London: David Fulton.

Rhodes, J. and Ajmal, Y. (1995) *Solution-Focused Thinking in Schools: Behaviour, Reading and Organisation*. London: BT Press.

Website

www.spiritwire.com/selfesteemquotes.html

References

Breakwell, G. (1997) *Coping with Aggressive Behaviour*. Leicester: British Psychological Society.

Cooley, C. (1902) *Human Nature and the Social Order*. New York: Charles Scribner's Sons.

Coopersmith, S. (1967) *The Antecedents of Self-Esteem*. San Francisco: Freeman Press.

De Shazer, S. (1985) *Keys to Solution in Brief Therapy.* New York: Norton.

Department for Children, Schools and Families (2005a) *Primary National Strategy: Focusing on Solutions: A Positive Approach to Improving Behaviour.* http://national strategies.standards.dcsf.gov.uk/node/86957.

Department for Children, Schools and Families (2005b) *Social and Emotional Aspects of Learning.* http://nationalstrategies.standards.dcsf.gov.uk/secondary/ behaviourattendanceandseal/secondaryseal.

Elmer, N. (2001) *Self-Esteem: The Costs and Causes of Low Self-Worth*. York: YPS.

Faupel, A., Herrick, E. and Sharp, P. (1998) *Anger Management: A Practical Guide.* London: David Fulton.

Furedi, F. (2004) *Therapy Culture: Cultivating Uncertainty in an Uncertain Age.* London: Routledge.

Hornby, G. (2003) 'Teachers and counselling', in C. Hall, E. Hall, G. Hornby (eds), *Counselling Pupils in School: Skills and Strategies for Teachers.* London: RoutledgeFalmer.

Lawrence, D. (2006) *Enhancing Self-Esteem in the Classroom*. London: Paul Chapman.

Mosley, J. and Tew, M. (1999) *Quality Circle Time in the Secondary School: A Handbook of Good Practice.* London: David Fulton.

Parker, M. (2009) 'Self-esteem', in M. Parker C. Lee, S. Gunn et al., *A Toolkit for the Effective Teaching Assistant*, 2nd edn. London: Sage.

7

The positive TA

This chapter is both a summary and a collection of ideas that draw together some concepts and themes. By the end of the chapter you will have considered and gained a better understanding of:

- what being positive means through seven key points;
- what you have learned from each of the exercises;
- what you have distilled from each of the exercises in terms of your thinking;
- what you have distilled from each of the exercises in terms of your practice;
- some final comments for positive TAs.

This summary chapter looks at important advice arising from the previous chapters that needs stating or emphasising. It aims to bring your learning into focus before some final statements in the conclusion.

This book has been about the skills, attitudes and approaches of TAs in a school setting. It recognises a simple truth, stated earlier in the book, which is that all you have control over is yourself, therefore it follows that maximising what you have is the best way to move forward professionally.

Unfortunately there is no equivalent programme for TAs in preparation for the classroom to that which teachers have access to. The HLTA has gone part of the way to alleviating the problem of professional development for some but many TAs are reliant on local authority professional development courses and Foundation Degree study, plus whatever may be provided in the school. There are few examples of training prior to starting work and it is often the case that from day one of their employment a TA will be in a classroom looking to their colleagues for solutions and relying on the good practice from their own past. This book has aimed to offer skills that can help prevent problems but more importantly has considered the importance of values and beliefs to how we react when life in the classroom becomes challenging. The three approaches from Chapters 4, 5 and 6 are not as self-contained as presented here because there is crossover between them. Their aim is to provide ideas and understanding that help the TA feel comfortable with their reactions when authority and order are challenged. Such comfort helps to reduce stress and increase effectiveness. With confidence in skills comes a more positive 'can do' approach to highly complex situations, and how you feel about your skills and how you think others see you responding will determine your sense of self-worth. The positive, confident TA possesses other attributes that help make their life at school and home a rewarding one.

Avoid perfection

One of the most destructive forces can be the 'be perfect' driver that some people possess, which means they have to go through life always getting things right all the time, always looking and behaving properly and never making mistakes. Perfection in some areas may be an ambition but if it is constantly demanded of yourself then it is a negative force. It is important that you allow yourself to make mistakes, indeed view doing so as part of the learning process that all adults (and children) in schools need to experience. It is good practice to license pupils to make mistakes so why not apply the practice to yourself? Take the blame for things that go wrong if you have contributed to it but avoid punishing yourself. There will be another chance to get it right next time. Also, remember when dealing with a difficult situation to develop a positive relationship, and get acknowledgement from pupils and peers that you deserve to say 'well done' to yourself – take the blame for that too! The TA who says 'I'm sorry Ben, I made a mistake explaining that, but I will make sure I do a better job of it next time' is a powerful model for their pupils.

Avoid negative focus

Because many support staff find themselves working with children and young people experiencing difficulties in school it is hard not to be problem focused and, even worse, concentrate on all the things that go wrong. Most of the day may be spent working well with appreciative staff and pupils but this can get lost when a negative incident happens. Most of the pupils behave well most of the time and most of your days at work go well. It is important to see your role as not defined by occasional problems, upsets and crises and more by the support you bring the pupils, staff and school or college.

Avoid problem adoption

It is all too easy to become so involved in the problems of the pupils that they become your problems too and such proximity prevents you becoming a problem-solver. Hard though it is at times your physical and psychological well-being is not best served by problem adoption. Taking time out, remembering others outside school who need you and love you and ensuring that you manage the school day in such a way that energy and patience levels are given time and the opportunity to regenerate will all help.

Avoid the single answer

One of the main aims of this book has been to suggest that what you think and believe will affect the way you deal with disruption. Your thoughts and beliefs are not stagnant and confined and, through your own professional development, you will see and understand alternatives and new ways of thinking and acting. Discovering new ideas and seeing how they relate to your beliefs will help to widen the range of skills and approaches adopted, and give you the potential to see that there is not one answer but a variety of them.

Enhancing pupil confidence (and perhaps your own)

The development of confidence is not easy and is more likely to arise from pupils achieving in practical tasks than through praise. Maclean (2003) suggests that improved confidence is achieved through a number of ways including the following:

- Pupils should be helped to understand that ability is not fixed and can change for the better.

- Success can be obtained in many different ways.

- Mistakes should be seen as ways of moving towards eventual achievement.

- Mistakes can be repaired.

- Effort should be acknowledged and pupils should be helped to realise that progress and effort are linked.

- Pupils should judge their progress at a personal level, not against the standards of others.

Sometimes adults find themselves praising the pupil unrealistically and focusing on the pupil's ability rather than their efforts. Rather than praise that might or might not be accurate there needs to be a recognition of how hard the pupil has tried, that they are worthy and are valued. From this basis some careful criticism will not dent their feelings of self and their desire to learn. While much of the above thinking would appear to apply to learning it applies equally to behaviour.

Remember behaviour is learned and purposeful

Whether inside or outside of school the behaviours that pupils exhibit are those which they have learned and are reactions to what is happening in a specific context. The aim of behaviour is to get certain needs met and it is important to understand that behaviour has a purpose. This is good news because it means that old, bad learned behaviours can be replaced by new, socially acceptable learned behaviours. If you look beyond what is happening and how the behaviour appears and try to see what the behaviour is trying to tell you it will increase your understanding and help you to make a better response.

Focusing on key learning and school achievement

At the heart of this book has been the link between one's values and beliefs and how that informs what we do in the classroom. In the ever expanding area of support work in schools and colleges, there is a need for staff to be aware of a variety of approaches to dealing with classroom management, not just the everyday difficulties that arise but also the more extreme reactions of some pupils. Professional development for TAs has become a key feature of good schools and there is always the personal desire that so many TAs possess to enhance their knowledge and skills. However, having worked on large numbers of professional development programmes with support staff and teachers, two questions emerge: first, what difference will this have made to the classroom experience and, second, what will they be able to take back to the school? With regard to the first point, staff sometimes adopt a small idea from a course or a specific approach without gaining the deeper understanding behind it. What that results in is a short-term effect without extensive changes to ideas or practice. Without the reasoning and understanding behind a concept there is the risk of being greeted with the cynical 'oh look who's been on a course', and often really good ideas and practices fall by the wayside when it comes to putting them into practice in the long term. With regard to the second point, some schools have highly sophisticated approaches and rigid, yet seemingly successful, systemic approaches for dealing with disruption, and the TA could find their new ideas do not blend in with prevailing practice.

The final two exercises in this book aim to focus on what has been learned through reading it, trying out ideas and engaging with the exercises. They also seek to focus on what difference new or enhanced practice can achieve in your school. The central belief that underpins them is that reflecting on what you have learned provides a chance to focus, refine and evaluate your practice, which is a rarity in modern school life.

 ## Exercise 7.1   Time to reflect

Below is a list of the exercises (number and their title).

1. In the third column tick if you have undertaken the exercise.

2. In the fourth column briefly list the key points you learned from the exercise.

3. In the fifth column consider what changes, based on the exercises, you may want to bring to your classroom practice or your school.

No.	Exercise title	Undertaken	Key points learned	What can be achieved in my school
1.1	The advantages of being a TA			
1.2	The disadvantages of being a TA			
2.1	Assessing my skills			
2.2	Influences on the behaviour of a known pupil			
3.1	The beliefs inventory			
3.2	The difference that TAs make			
4.1	Evaluation of the system			
4.2	Quadrant analysis			
4.3	The important features of rules			
4.4	What are your views on punishment?			
4.5	Your consequence statements			
5.1	Negotiation questions sheet			

(Continued)

(Continued)

5.2	Does work, could work or perhaps does not work			
6.1	Masks your pupils put on			
6.2	Powerful quotations			
6.3	Working on self-esteem			

Exercise 7.2   Time to act

1. From your answers to question 2 in Exercise 7.1 choose *three* essential things that have greatly influenced your thinking (probably from the 'Key points learned' column).

    (a)
    (b)
    (c)

    How will they influence your practice?

2. From your answers to question 3 in Exercise 7.1 choose *three* essential things that have greatly influenced your hopes for your practice.

    (a)
    (b)
    (c)

    How will you bring them into your classroom practice? Who else might gain from such ideas?

Conclusion

In describing how important it is for teachers to keep matters in perspective Rogers (2009) uses the visual metaphor of a dot in a white box and the need to see that the white box is bigger than the black dot, even though the black dot keeps our focus and is sometimes all that is seen. This metaphor also applies *to you*, whatever your role in supporting the learning of young people. Even if the dot appears to be growing bigger and is all that you can see, look for ways to make the white space larger through the support of colleagues and friends and your capacity to develop new ideas and refine old ones that always worked before.

Whenever writing about challenging, disruptive or confrontational behaviour it is easy to fall into the trap of forgetting how well behaved and orderly most of the pupils are for most of the time. On the rare days when things go wrong, they rarely go totally wrong, but it becomes hard to see the sunshine behaviour of your pupils and your colleagues because you feel you have been riding out the black storm caused by the disruption of a few or even just one individual. It is at this time that you need to remind yourself of what you have achieved, that you might have made mistakes (which is permitted) and that your beliefs and values that you have made clear to yourself show that you are a professional who has a capacity to learn new skills and ideas, and also to gain a deeper understanding of all that you do. The aim of this book has been to assist that professional development in a supportive, informative and practical way, to enhance what you do and what you think when you deal with children or young people who are or have been disruptive and challenging and, beyond that, to increase your understanding of yourself.

References

Maclean, A. (2003) *The Motivated School*. London: Paul Chapman.
Rogers, B. (2009) 'Principles and practices that enable us to make a difference with individual children and classroom groups', in *How to Manage Children's Challenging Behaviour*, 2nd edn. London: Paul Chapman Publishing.

Index